How to Say It
Performance Reviews

52 - 1 min documentation process (pre work)
69 - 1 min Manager prep worksheet
15 - definition of review
16 - Job Desc. vs Job Goal
19 - Feedback (listening)
20 - 5 step (in person) review SOP

HOW TO SAY IT

Performance Reviews

Phrases and Strategies for Painless and Productive Performance Reviews

Meryl Runion *and* Janelle Brittain

PRENTICE HALL PRESS

A PRENTICE HALL BOOK
Published by the Penguin Group
Penguin Group (USA) Inc.
375 Hudson Street, New York, New York 10014, USA
Penguin Group (Canada), 90 Eglinton Avenue East, Suite 700, Toronto, Ontario M4P 2Y3,
Canada (a division of Pearson Penguin Canada Inc.)
Penguin Books Ltd., 80 Strand, London WC2R 0RL, England
Penguin Group Ireland, 25 St. Stephen's Green, Dublin 2, Ireland
(a division of Penguin Books Ltd.)
Penguin Group (Australia), 250 Camberwell Road, Camberwell, Victoria 3124, Australia
(a division of Pearson Australia Group Pty. Ltd.)
Penguin Books India Pvt. Ltd., 11 Community Centre, Panchsheel Park, New Delhi—110 017,
India
Penguin Group (NZ), Cnr. Airborne and Rosedale Roads, Albany, Auckland 1310,
New Zealand (a division of Pearson New Zealand Ltd.)
Penguin Books (South Africa) (Pty.) Ltd., 24 Sturdee Avenue, Rosebank, Johannesburg 2196,
South Africa

Penguin Books Ltd., Registered Offices: 80 Strand, London WC2R 0RL, England

While the author has made every effort to provide accurate telephone numbers and Internet
addresses at the time of publication, neither the publisher nor the author assumes any responsibility for errors, or for changes that occur after publication. Further, the publisher does
not have any control over and does not assume any responsibility for author or third-party
websites or their content.

First edition: December 2006

Library of Congress Cataloging-in-Publication Data

Runion, Meryl.
   How to say it performance reviews : phrases and strategies for painless and productive
performance reviews / Meryl Runion and Janelle Brittain.— 1st ed.
     p.   cm. — (How to say it)
   "A Prentice Hall Book."
   ISBN 0-7352-0412-8
   1. Employees—Rating of. 2. Performance—Terminology. 3. Employees—Rating
of—Terminology. I. Brittain, Jan. II. Title.

HF5549.5.R3R86   2006
658.3'125—dc22

2006030149

PRINTED IN THE UNITED STATES OF AMERICA

10 9 8 7 6 5 4 3 2 1

Most Prentice Hall Books are available at special quantity discounts for bulk purchases for
sales promotions, premiums, fund-raising, or educational use. Special books, or book ex-
cerpts, can also be created to fit specific needs. For details, write: Special Markets, The Berkley
Publishing Group, 375 Hudson Street, New York, New York 10014.

Acknowledgments

In addition to our enormous and heartfelt generic appreciation (Mom, Dad, our first grade teachers—you know the drill), we want to thank our agent, Barry Neville, for getting this project rolling. Thanks to Mike Scott of Mike Scott & Associates (www.totallyaccountable.com) for working with Meryl on this manuscript at its commencement. Special appreciation goes to Kris Porotsky at A Second Pair of Eyes for her excellent proofreading skills.

Patricia Hubbard from the law firm of Seyfarth Shaw, LLP, in Chicago, provided us with insightful counsel on the legal chapter. We are grateful to her for making certain we steer you correctly. Michael Wynne of International Management Consulting Associates in Chicago was a tremendous help adding his creativity and humor to our bonus superlative phrases.

Disclaimer

This book is designed to provide performance review advice and guidance. Every effort was made to provide advice that is accurate, sound, and useful. This book is not intended to provide specific legal advice or to be a substitute for seeking legal counsel. The publisher and authors cannot be held liable or responsible for any damages caused or allegedly caused directly or indirectly by the information in this book.

Contents

PHRASE CATEGORIES ORGANIZED BY TOPIC

Interpersonal and Team Skills: Chapter 15

Management and Leadership Skills: Chapter 16

Task and Technical Skills: Chapter 17

Professionalism: Chapter 18

PHRASE CATEGORIES ORGANIZED ALPHABETICALLY

What They Never Tell You About Performance Reviews

1

What They Told You About Performance Reviews Is Wrong

Sad But True: A Myopic Performance Review

Jim was one of those employees that companies love to hire, keep, and promote. He had a great attitude, did whatever it took to get the job done, came in early, and left late when necessary. When managers needed someone to take on an important project and do it right, they turned to Jim first.

This year was as stellar as the previous years. While Jim recently made a minor error on the completion date of an order, he corrected the error immediately, and his boss seemed unconcerned. Jim saw no reason to worry about his upcoming performance review. There was nothing to prepare him for what was about to happen when his boss casually said, "Jim, it's that time of year again. I guess we just have to get your review over with before HR gets on my case about it."

Jim walked into his boss's office and took a seat as usual. Without looking at Jim, Jim's boss nervously made small talk, put his glasses on, pulled out the official performance

review form, and began to read how he had "rated" Jim in the
prescribed areas of the form. Then the bomb fell. Jim's boss
read a statement about Jim's miserable failure on a recent or-
der and told Jim that error not only disqualified him for pro-
motion in the department, but it would go on his permanent
record. Jim's attempts to defend his performance were stifled,
and his boss abruptly ended the meeting by saying he had
other employees to review.

Jim's boss refused to meet again to discuss the review, and
HR handled Jim's objections by placing his rebuttal letter
into his personnel file.

Jim stopped coming in early or staying late. Coworkers
noticed the change as Jim began to look for a job in another
company.

A few well-worded phrases could have transformed
Jim's review into an empowering positive experience.
Instead, Jim's boss turned a star employee into a marginal performer, because everything Jim's boss thought
he knew about performance reviews was wrong. Jim's
experience is as unfortunate as it is common. Performance reviews are dreaded because of common management misconceptions that not only cause the process to
fail but cause it to be highly destructive.

I'D RATHER HAVE A ROOT CANAL: THE TEN MANAGER MISCONCEPTIONS THAT MAKE PERFORMANCE REVIEWS A DREADED AND PAINFUL ORDEAL

We've taught hundreds of management seminars, and
we rarely find managers who look forward to perfor-

mance reviews. When we suggest it is even possible for performance reviews to be positive experiences, the room is often filled with moans and groans. That's because everything most managers think they know about performance reviews is wrong. There are ten management misconceptions about performance reviews that are responsible for making them dreaded and painful ordeals.

Manager Misconception #1: "I'm a manager; therefore I'm a 'performance review natural.'"

You come into life knowing how to breathe, and you come into life knowing how to cry. You don't need anyone to show you how to do those things. You do not come into life knowing how to conduct a performance review. Yet companies and managers casually perform reviews with little training, expecting managers to magically know how to conduct them. While a poorly delivered review is rarely fatal to managers or employees, it can be fatal to careers. A poorly delivered performance review can result in poor performance, contagious low morale, and unnecessary turnover. Managers need to be trained in how to conduct reviews that bolster productivity, relationships, commitment, and effectiveness.

Manager Misconception #2: "The way I was reviewed was good enough for me, so it'll be good enough for my people."

Your first performance reviews came from your parents. Later in your life you were reviewed by teachers and coaches, and then by the bosses who learned to conduct reviews from their early experiences. Managers rarely question the approaches that were modeled to them, and they continue to do unto others what was done unto them. Here's a news flash! The reviews you received may not be a good role model to follow.

Manager Misconception #3: "Performance reviews don't matter."

Never underestimate the power of performance reviews. Performance reviews affect an employee's pay, career, morale, job performance, attendance, promotions, families, employee turnover, and so much more. Performance reviews can be used in court against managers and against companies who conduct them poorly. Performance reviews can be used in discrimination cases against a company or manager. These cases and lawsuits can cost hundreds of thousands of dollars to settle and/or win.

Not only is there potential harm in a poorly conducted review, there also is a missed opportunity for employee accountability, satisfaction, and renewed commitment as well as a missed opportunity for company growth. When you take employees up to another level of performance, the company goes, too. Performance reviews matter.

Manager Misconception #4: "Performance reviews are just paperwork exercises."

Performance reviews are not just busywork, unless you make them that. A properly delivered performance review can be a powerful catalyst for improving behavior and performance. Go beyond paperwork and focus on excellence.

Manager Misconception #5: "Performance reviews are a one-way, top-down process."

There was a time when performance reviews were authoritatively administered to passive, subservient, and uninvolved employees. The workplace has changed! These days the process is a manager-employee *partnership*, which creates greater buy-in, more motivation, and higher levels of performance. Because companies must outperform their competition, their employees must outperform last year's accomplishments. Not only is communication two-way these days; often employees are asked to review the management approach of their boss.

Manager Misconception #6: "It's us against them."

If you conduct reviews with an adversarial, "me versus them" attitude, you'll immediately trigger blistering defensiveness. A defensive employee is likely to become demotivated and angry and is likely to resist making any changes. See yourself as an ally, a guide, and a coach to help employees be successful, and help your employees to see you that way.

Manager Misconception #7: "Reviews are about my opinion."

We all have opinions, but the performance review is not the place to offer yours. It's not a matter of whether you like the person or not. Every word you speak in your reviews must be based on measurable goals, results, and concrete, observable behavior. Talk about behaviors, re-sults, and actions, and steer clear of opinions. Your be-liefs and opinions as a manager have no place in the review.

Manager Misconception # 8: "Performance reviews are payback time."

Some managers see reviews as an opportunity to get even with an employee who has caused them frustration throughout the year. If you play "I gotcha" with an em-ployee, there's a good chance the employee will find a way to "getcha" back. Handle performance issues in the coaching and counseling process throughout the year, and avoid any temptation to ambush an employee in the review.

Manager Misconception # 9: "I can do reviews from memory."

You've got a lot on your mind. Work is packed with de-tails, interactions, and commitments to remember. Make it easy on yourself: document throughout the year. If you try to do your reviews from memory, your review is likely to overfocus on the previous sixty days and over-look important employee contributions throughout the year. Base your reviews on observations of trends based on facts recorded in a performance tracking system.

Manager Misconception #10: "I can check off boxes and sign the form just before the employee walks into the meeting."

Yes, we know, your life is busy, but—sorry—reviews are too important to do them off the cuff. You need to offer concrete examples from the entire performance period to back up your praise or constructive feedback. That requires consistent documentation and advanced preparation. It requires an investment in time that will save time in management issues throughout the year.

Manager Misconception Checklist

Check the misconceptions you need to overcome:

❑ **MANAGER MISCONCEPTION #1:** "I'm a manager; therefore I'm a 'performance review natural.'"

❑ **MANAGER MISCONCEPTION #2:** "The way I was reviewed was good enough for me, so it'll be good enough for my people."

❑ **MANAGER MISCONCEPTION #3:** "Performance reviews don't matter."

☑ **MANAGER MISCONCEPTION #4:** "Performance reviews are just paperwork exercises."

❑ **MANAGER MISCONCEPTION #5:** "Performance reviews are a one-way, top-down process."

❑ **MANAGER MISCONCEPTION #6:** "It's us against them."

❑ **MANAGER MISCONCEPTION #7:** "Reviews are about my opinion."

❑ **MANAGER MISCONCEPTION #8:** "Performance reviews are payback time."

☑ **MANAGER MISCONCEPTION #9:** "I can do reviews from memory."

❑ **MANAGER MISCONCEPTION #10:** "I can check off boxes and sign the form just before the employee walks into the meeting."

The following chapters will help you address these and many other issues to advance your performance management skills. These tools will guide you to inspire your team members to meet and surpass their goals.

2

The Five Essential Processes of the Totally Integrated Performance System (TIPS)

TIPS TO ACHIEVE EVERY MANAGER'S DREAM: EMPLOYEE ACCOUNTABILITY

A TIPS Turnaround

Mike, a new manager in his department, quickly realized he'd walked into a hornet's nest. He was continually getting complaints from his people that others in the department were stepping on each other's territory, they were going off in different directions, and he was concerned about the accuracy and quality of much of the work that came out of the department. To top it all off, when he looked at last year's performance reviews, there were just boxes checked with no notes, no development plans, and everyone was rated as "Acceptable."

This gave Mike a real-world application to apply the TIPS approach he had learned about at his old job. He began by

*setting appointments with each of his staff to review and
clarify their job descriptions. He had to iron out some issues
between a couple of people, but it was an important clarifying process. Another part of the job clarification was to analyze how each person contributed to the company goals.*

*Mike committed himself to giving immediate feedback to
staff when they performed above or below standard. After
each conversation he quickly documented the interaction and
put it in the staff's file. Rather than waiting until year end
for the performance review, at the end of each month he held
an interim review with each person to discuss their progress
on their goals, analyze any trends in their performance, and
agree on performance plans for the next month. Mike's team
quickly learned he was serious about expecting top-level performance. He was proud of his team at the end of the year
when he gave performance reviews. Each person had at least
some categories he could genuinely rate as exceptional performance.*

*Mike turned his department around by implementing TIPS
in his department. TIPS is a Totally Integrated Performance
System, a five-step process of performance management that
culminates in the performance review. Every step supports
every other step. By using this process you can obtain what
Mike did and what every manager wants: accountable employees.*

THE TOTALLY INTEGRATED PERFORMANCE SYSTEM: THE FIVE ESSENTIAL TIPS PROCESSES

Five processes are essential to the totally integrated performance review.

TIPS Process #1: Job Clarification and Goal Alignment

Review each job description to make sure it follows the three Rs, and *really reflects reality*.

Throughout the year, revisit how each responsibility is described and add or subtract responsibilities to keep the description accurate. Descriptions should paint a clear picture of what that responsibility is like when it is performed at 100 percent. Review the examples below.

> **UNCLEAR:** "Answers the phone."
> **CLEAR: "Answers the phone with the correct company greeting in a cheerful, welcoming voice."**
> **UNCLEAR:** "Completes reports."
> **CLEAR: "Completes reports with 100 percent accuracy and turns them in before 5:00 each Friday."**

Provide detail of what the responsibility sounds like or looks like when done exactly how you want it.

Clarify employee goals by breaking each company goal into specific, measurable steps for each department or team. Present this plan to employees for input to establish individual goals that synthesize company goals and job descriptions.

The job description is the foundation for the entire performance process, and employee goals create focus on successfully meeting job requirements. Be sure your employees' job descriptions and employee goals clearly and accurately reflect the requirements of their jobs as determined by the goals of the organization.

TIPS Process #2: Consistent Performance Tracking

Establish a working file for each employee. The working file should include the One-Minute Documentation notes you take throughout the year (see chapter 6). Record the details of all of the employee's significant accomplishments and shortcomings in the working file. Be sure to include any letters of compliments or complaints as well. Include any other documents that are examples of the points made in your notes.

TIPS Process #3: Interim Performance Reviews

Schedule interim performance reviews monthly or at least quarterly to keep employees focused on making progress toward goals and to keep employees informed. This will help you to avoid surprises at the year-end reviews. Track performance and support progress by coaching. Keep records of these meetings in the working file. This consistent and frequent focus lets the employees know you are serious about them meeting their goals and that you are there to help them.

TIPS Process #4: Address Performance Problems with a Plan (As Needed)

If performance problems remain despite coaching, schedule a performance improvement meeting to design and implement a plan to correct the performance issue. Don't wait until the annual performance review to address recurring issues. Counsel the employee in conjunction with the company's progressive discipline process. Keep records of these meetings in the working file.

TIPS Process #5: Pull It All Together in the Formal Performance Review.
The formal performance review compares the job description and the goals from process #1 with the performance documented in the working file. Use practiced scripting with documented supporting details to summarize the accomplishments of the employee during the specified performance period. Then work with the employee to establish new goals for the coming year.

TIPS: PRINCIPLES BEHIND THE PROCESS

Here are some essential principles necessary for the TIPS process to be successful:

- The president is the major supporting force behind effective and timely reviews.
- The president always reviews the executives and vice versa.
- Effective training is given to support the importance and process of preparing and presenting effective and powerful reviews.
- Pay raises, if available, are given only to those employees who have earned them.
- Cost-of-living increases are also given only to those employees who have earned them.
- Employees are kept informed throughout the year of their progress to avoid surprises at reviews.

THE DIFFERENCE BETWEEN JOB STANDARDS AND JOB GOALS

Distinguish between the job standards in the job description and individual performance goals. The job description establishes essential job functions that would apply to anyone who held that position. In addition to these standards, set performance goals for each employee. Goals to meet standards are essential goals. Goals to exceed standards are elective goals.

For example, for an employee who needs minimal computer skills in their job, a goal to develop those minimal skills is an essential goal to meet job standards. If this employee sets a goal to develop computer skills beyond what the job requires, that goal is an elective goal. When the employee does not meet elective goals, don't penalize the employee in the review rating. Rate them as "Meeting Expectations" or "Acceptable." When the employee does not meet an essential goal, mention that failure in the review as "Not Meeting Expectations" or "Needs Improvement."

HOW THE FIRST FOUR TIPS PROCESSES SET A FOUNDATION FOR THE PERFECT FORMAL PERFORMANCE REVIEW

If you faithfully implement TIPS processes #1 to #4, the formal annual or semiannual performance review will be an effortless and painless process. The first four steps lay the groundwork that allows the formal review process to be what it was designed to be: an accurate reflection of the successes of the performance period and the opportunity to create a plan for greater success in the performance period to come.

Your TIPS Checklist

Check off the TIPS practices you intend to add to your current approach.

- ❏ Update job descriptions, making sure they *really reflect reality*.
- ❏ Make sure job descriptions describe what each responsibility looks like when performed at 100 percent.
- ❏ Determine that employee's responsibilities and goals are aligned with organizational goals.
- ❏ Maintain a working file with specific detailed records to support reviews.
- ❏ Provide monthly or at least quarterly interim reviews.
- ❏ Provide coaching and/or progressive discipline between reviews, as needed.
- ❏ Use practiced phrases to convey your messages clearly (see chapters 15–18, pages 107–203)
- ❏ Provide and receive training in the process of preparing for and presenting powerful reviews.
- ❏ Keep employees informed throughout the year to avoid surprises at the year-end review.

3

The Five Steps
of a Masterful
Performance Review

THE IMPORTANCE OF PROPER PHRASING
FOR EVERY STAGE OF THE REVIEW

Does it matter how you say hello? Does it matter how you close? Yes and yes. It is well known that people remember the first and last thing they see or hear. Most managers focus on the details of the evaluation, which are important. But it is also important to set the right tone before plunging into specifics and to end the conversation in a way that motivates the employee to take action. If you focus only on the evaluative part of the review and neglect other aspects, it could undermine the impact of the review. Prepare yourself for every aspect of the review.

WHY AND HOW TO INVITE FEEDBACK AT EVERY STAGE OF THE REVIEW

Most managers wait until the end of their presentation of the review to solicit feedback, if they solicit feedback at all. Naturally, the bulk of the feedback will come once all the information is on the table, but ideally, the entire review will be a two-way conversation about performance. That's why we do not have soliciting feedback as a separate stage of the review. We advocate soliciting feedback throughout, so employees feel heard and so they do self-analysis. The more employees feel heard, the more able they will be to hear what you say. The more self-analysis employees do, the more they will take ownership for their behavior and for the goals you establish. Some phrases to solicit feedback are:

- I invite your input at any point in the review.
- How does that sound to you?
- Did I make that clear to you?
- Did you have a comment about that?
- What would you like to say about that point?
- How does your evaluation of your performance align with mine?
- I understand that you don't agree with what I've said. While I appreciate your input, I haven't heard anything that changes my evaluation.

THE FIVE-STEP PERFORMANCE REVIEW PROCESS

Step 1: Greet the Employee

Set the Tone

There is a saying that "well begun is half done." While that might be a bit optimistic, your opening remarks do set the tone for the entire interview. Pick three words to describe the tone you want to set, and choose your opening words to create that tone. For example, you may choose the words "supportive," "efficient," and "focused." Or perhaps you will choose the words "straightforward," "effective," and "productive." Having words to define the tone will help you know what phrases you will want to select in your opening to the review.

Relax and Connect

Generally we recommend you start with a minute or two of small talk. Less is impersonal, and if you chat longer, your employee may get impatient and think you are avoiding the issue. A brief comment or two can create a connection between you and relax tensions. Start with remarks like:

- Have you recovered from the push to complete the Gibbons proposal?
- Can you believe we had an emergency drill in this weather?

Clearly, these examples are situation specific. If you can't get any more specific than commenting on the weather, then go ahead and comment on the weather, but the best small talk phrases are ones that are specific to your employee or shared experiences.

Step 2: Set Expectations

There is a saying in the speaking and training industries that applies to performance reviews as well. It says: ["Tell them what you're going to tell them, tell them what you said you would tell them, and then tell them what you told them."] Set expectations to create ease and enhance focus. You know how you plan to proceed, but it is important that they know the agenda as well.

Some useful phrases are:

- We are here today to review how you did your job since your last review.
- It's a chance for me to acknowledge your accomplishments and for us to see where there is room or a need for improvement.
- We are here today to review the successes and lessons learned from last year and to make plans for next year.

Next, focus on the agenda:

- Here's how our hour together will go. First, I will give you the summary of your review. Next, we will look at your strongest points in detail. Then, we will see where you can improve. After that, we will look forward to goals for the coming period. Finally, we will discuss follow-up.

This is a good point to use phrases that solicit feedback, such as:

- This review is for and about you, so I'd like for it to sound more like a dialogue than a lecture from me.
- I invite your comments as you think of them.

Let them know how you summarize performance.

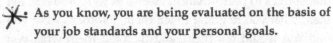

- As you know, you are being evaluated on the basis of your job standards and your personal goals.
- We have ten criteria of primary focus. They are . . .
- There are three ratings. They are: "Exceptional," "Acceptable," and "Needs Improvement."

Step 3: Summarize Performance

Refer to section IV of this book for detailed performance phrases.

Strengths

We recommend you start with strengths, rather than go through the performance criteria in a random order. Your employee will be more open to hearing about areas of weakness if his or her strengths have already been acknowledged.

We combine the "Exceptional" and "Acceptable" phrases in section IV because the difference between exceptional and acceptable performance is usually a matter of frequency and degree. For instance, an "exceptionally adaptable employee" may consistently and immediately see change as an opportunity, while an "acceptably adaptable employee" may resist change briefly and then embrace it. Adapt the phrases to your situation with adjectives that indicate the frequency and degree you see the characteristics you are rating.

Address strengths in four parts:

1. **Summary Phrase:** Summarize the rating and the strength using sentence stems such as:

   - In the area of _____ I rated you _____. Specifically . . .

2. **Documentation/Example Phrase:** Document the success by data and example using sentence stems such as:

   - This is demonstrated by . . .
   - An example is . . .
   - On (date) you . . .
   - For example . . .
   - This quality is shown by . . .

3. **Impact Phrase:** Communicate the impact of that success using sentence stems such as:

   - Here's why your great performance is so valuable . . .
   - Because of what you did we were able to . . .
   - This causes . . .
   - The benefit of this was . . .
   - Your performance also affects . . .

4. **Action Phrase:** Explain how you would like that skill applied more in the future.

   - I'd like to see more of . . .
   - You're so good in this area, I can see you . . .
   - This opens up possibilities for . . .

Here's an example of the four parts of relaying strengths:

1. **Summary Phrase:**

   • Your rating on accuracy is "highly accurate."

2. **Documentation/Example Phrase:**

   • I was particularly impressed with how you quickly caught a major error in the business plan others overlooked.

3. **Impact Phrase:**

   • That catch prevented us from wasting hundreds of business hours going down the wrong road.

4. **Action Phrase:**

   • I invite you to continue to advise us of overlooked errors in the future.

Areas that Need Improvement

Discuss all areas for improvements at once to increase focus on what change or growth is needed. Please note: if you really don't see an area of deficiency, you don't need to invent one or pretend one exists. Transition to the discussion of weaker areas by saying:

• There are some areas that need improvement.
• Now let's look at some areas that need development.
• Next, let's look at some areas where I know you can perform better.

Relay weakness in five steps:

1. **Summary Phrase:** Summarize the rating and the problem using a phrase such as:

   - **In the area of _____ I rated you "needs improvement." Specifically . . .**

   (Refer to chapters 15–18 for phrases to define the performance.)

2. **Documentation/Example Phrase:** Document the problem by example.

   - **I chose this rating because of incidents like the following . . .**
   - **For example, the other day I noticed . . .**
   - **We've already discussed examples of this, but to remind you, some examples are . . .**

3. **Impact Phrase:** Point out the impact of the weakness.

   - **This is a problem because . . .**
   - **This resulted in . . .**
   - **This causes . . .**

4. **Action Phrase:** Specifically describe what the employee needs to do, instead of what they were doing. Describe what performance looks or sounds like when performed at 100 percent.

   - **To turn this around, I suggest you . . .**
   - **What I need you to start doing is . . .**
   - **What I need you to stop doing is . . .**

5. **Gain Agreement:** After you describe the problems with the old performance and establish what new

behavior is needed, gain acknowledgment from the employee that they understand the problem and agreement that they are committed to making the changes. Some phrases to solicit agreement are:

- Do you see that the impact of your performance can cause these problems?
- Do you understand what you need to do to improve your performance?
- Do you have any ideas on what you can do to improve your performance?
- How will you implement this change?

Here's an example of how to communicate areas for improvement in five parts:

1. **Summary Phrase:** Your rating on accomplishing tasks is "Needs improvement: Does not anticipate and plan for problems."
2. **Documentation/Example Phrase:** One example is with the Raines proposal. You budgeted your time without allotting time for glitches.
3. **Impact Phrase:** That resulted in the administrative support staff having to work overtime to meet the deadline. This cost the company $450 in overtime fees and caused two staff members to have to take time away from their families.
4. **Action Phrase:** Your planning needs to be brought up to the same level as your communication skills. To correct this, I suggest that in the future you budget 20 percent extra time for problems that may arise.

5. **Gain Agreement Phrase:** Do you agree that allocating the extra time will work to resolve this problem?

The employee may offer other action suggestions that you can develop together.

Step 4: Look Forward

This section of the review is to discuss what happens from this point on. This is an optimal time to set goals. Some useful phrases are:

- **Now let's review the areas of strength and see how we can enhance those areas, and then look at the weaker areas to establish improvement goals for the future.**
- Now that we know where we are, let's take a look at where we want to be and how to get there.
- Here's the level you are currently at in the area of (area). What do you see as a challenging but reasonable goal in that area?

Step 5: Close

The closing is your call to action. Use it to summarize agreements, restate goals, and reaffirm the relationship.

- I'm excited about the possibilities ahead.
- I'm glad we had this opportunity to meet.
- I think we've accomplished a lot in this hour, and I look forward to our continued working relationship.
- I want to leave you knowing how much we appreciate your work and how glad we are that you are here.

- I really appreciate your contributions this year, and I have full confidence in your abilities to meet next year's goals.

The closing also is your opportunity to inform the employee of what follow-up there will be and <u>how to file an objection to the review should that</u> be desired.

- The next step is that these forms will be filed with the Human Resources Department . . .
- We will meet at the end of each month to review your progress on your goals.
- I understand you do not agree with some points of my evaluation. Should you choose, the process to file an objection is to . . .

If you, like many managers, thought all you had to consider in the review was phrases for performance, this chapter provides another dimension to your review process. If you lose your employee's attention at "Hello," you'll probably be talking to yourself by the time you describe performance. If you prepare for every stage of the review, your performance reviews will not just meet but will surpass all expectations.

4

Why Timing Is Everything

Employees Don't Know if You Don't Tell Them

Judy's employee Bill missed deadlines and made mistakes in his work. Judy was under pressure and didn't want to take the time to talk to Bill. When something had a crucial deadline, Judy did the work herself or passed it on to someone she could count on, giving Bill work that was neither crucial nor time sensitive. This went on for months. Bill was unaware of Judy's issues, and he thought he was doing a terrific job.

At the formal performance review, Judy confronted Bill about his lack of quality work and missed deadlines. Bill was stunned and incredulous. When Bill asked for clarification, Judy could only recall a few incidents. Bill had no idea those incidents were problematic and was angry that he was not given the opportunity to explain his position at the time. Bill felt blindsided because Judy saved her feedback for the performance review.

THE IMPORTANCE OF TIMING IN FEEDBACK

Judy is not the only manager to wait until the performance review to address an issue or offer feedback. Many managers never address issues outside the performance review, and many others avoid the performance review entirely. Some managers think that casual comments qualify as performance reviews. They do not.

If you wait until the performance review to address issues or offer praise, you are being passive-aggressive, and you will undermine trust. If you wait until the performance review to address issues, you miss the opportunity to maximize performance. Your number one responsibility as a manager is to get your employees to do the job they are hired to do. That is impossible without appropriate, well-timed feedback.

WHAT TO DO WHEN: HOW TO TIME YOUR FEEDBACK

There is a saying, "It's not what you say, it's how you say it." The authors want to add that it's also *when* you say it. Here are some guidelines about feedback timing.

1. Provide immediate feedback about issues unless you are not in private. (Emergencies are an exception to the privacy guideline.)
2. If issues arise when you are not alone, find a private place to talk, or address the issues at your first opportunity.

3. Praise work well done immediately, whether you are in private or not.

4. Document both positive and negative incidents in the working file at the time of the occurrence.

5. Document feedback immediately after it is given. Use that documentation as the basis of the monthly interim performance reviews.

6. Use your monthly interim reviews as a foundation for yearly or twice-yearly formal reviews.

7. Have in-depth coaching meetings with employees with repeated performance issues that are not corrected by immediate feedback.

WHEN TO SCHEDULE PERFORMANCE REVIEWS

Unless your organization requires you to conduct reviews on a designated timetable, schedule your reviews at times when the workload is likely to be the lightest. You may choose to spread your reviews across the year to spread the workload out. That will allow you to focus better on each review.

Once the time is set for reviews, maintain that cycle within a thirty-day range.

If an employee is new, allow sufficient time (six months) for the employee to adjust. During this period, increase the number of informal feedback conversations and reviews.

If you are a new manager to an employee or team, allow at least six months to conduct a formal review so you have enough time to observe and gather information.

FREQUENCY OF REVIEWS

Performance review is one of the most important tools you have to recognize and improve the contributions and skills of the individuals who make up your organization. It is also an essential tool to plan for future success. Things change quickly in the work environment, which is why you need to conduct your review at least annually. More frequent reviews are useful, and less frequent reviews are discouraged.

TIME ALLOTMENT

Allow at least one hour per review.

WELL-TIMED FEEDBACK AVOIDS
PERFORMANCE REVIEW SURPRISES

A general guideline of performance reviews is that there should be no surprises. By following the TIPS procedures in great timing, not only will there be no surprises, but there will also be no disappointment.

5

You Gotta Know
the Law

A Defense Lawyer's Nightmare

It's an employment defense lawyer's nightmare, and a recurrent one for Paula. When Jill hired Paula to represent her regarding Roger's suspension, Jill assured her she had done everything properly. Jill told Paula that Roger had been her worst employee ever with a history of repeated mistakes and insufficiencies that led to his suspension. Jill was confident that Roger's grievance was baseless.

So why, Paula wondered, was there almost no documentation in the performance file, and why were Roger's previous reviews marked "Meets Expectations"? Paula knew that the judge would ask, "If Jill did not even take the time or trouble to document this issue, how bad could it have been?"

Paula also knew that without documentation Jill's case lacked credibility. People believe in documents, even if a manager can testify to the same thing. Paula had represented several clients in claims where the government investigator took the fact of documentation as proof of the event yet discredited or minimized oral testimony from a supervisor on the same events. While the law says there is no difference between the admissibility of oral testimony and written documentation, as a practical matter, paper speaks volumes.

Jill offered to draft documentation after the fact, but even if she had remembered the kind of details that were needed, retroactive documentation does not carry the impact of immediate documentation.

Because of the inadequate documentation, insufficient details, and past reviews marked "Meets expectations," Paula knew she had a tough case.

After reviewing the file, Paula told Jill what her options were. It was not what Jill wanted to hear. Paula said, "Because of the problems with the documentation, this case will be expensive and difficult to defend. I can fight it for you, but I recommend you revoke the suspension and document every performance issue from here on. Then if you need to suspend or discharge him in the future, you'll have what we need to make a case."

YOU DON'T HAVE TO GO TO JAIL, PAY A $50,000 FINE, OR REHIRE SOMEONE YOU JUST FIRED: THE TOP TEN DON'TS OF A PERFORMANCE REVIEW

Jill learned about performance review legal issues the hard way. Reading this chapter is a much easier way to learn. Mistakes in representing performance and misspeaking in a review can be costly. We asked Chicago employment attorney Patricia Hubbard of Seyfarth Shaw, LLP, to list ten things to avoid and six things to include in your performance reviews to minimize problematic employment legal challenges. These tips reduce the likelihood of your being faced with legal challenges, and they make defending your decisions easier if you are.

1. **Don't make statements that are not job-related or that delve into personal or protected areas during the review.** (Personal topics include personal life, disability, marriage issues, age, religion, pregnancy, etc.). Even a friendly inquiry into child care issues or about parents who are ill could be interpreted by the employee to be evidence of discrimination. Stick with issues related to the employee's performance and conduct in the workplace.

2. **Don't provide exclusively negative feedback.** Even where there are serious performance concerns, acknowledge the employee's contributions and positive efforts. If you only discuss the negative, it can be demoralizing and demotivating. Also, a review that only contains negatives makes a supervisor appear unfair, which often works against your company should you need to defend a claim.

3. **Don't raise your voice or be belittling.** The single most important thing you can do in supervising an employee—including providing reviews—is deliver information respectfully. If an employee feels his supervisor listens to his concerns, input, and requests, he is far less likely to respond negatively or with hostility when told of performance problems. The vast majority of employment court cases end up there because someone's feelings were hurt or because they thought they were treated unfairly. No one listens well or responds well to disrespectful

tones. Even bad news can be presented respectfully. Don't say anything that would unreasonably irritate you if your boss said it to you—the golden rule works in the workplace, too.

4. **Don't make promises you cannot deliver on**. It's dangerous to say, "This time next year, you'll be in a position to . . ." A more accurate statement would be, "The goals and improvements we set will increase your chances to be in a position to . . . this time next year."

5. **Don't comment on someone's poor attendance or interruption to operations if he was on protected leave, such as leave under the Family and Medical Leave Act.** If you make a comment about a protected leave, even if your comment is intended to be innocent, it could be regarded as an indication of discrimination. No matter how disruptive an employee's absences have been, avoid commenting if the absences are protected by law. Excessive absences that are not excused by law can be included in the review.

6. **Don't miss the opportunity to give feedback, even if things are running smoothly.** Saying, "You're doing fine, there is nothing really to discuss" unfairly cheats the high achiever of his rewards. There is always something to discuss, even if it is to clarify exactly what you appreciate about their performance. Employees love to hear things like, "I really like how you anticipate my need to prepare month-end reports by organizing the sales data as it comes in." Discuss the goals for next year and new challenges

for high performers as well. Don't let them get bored—provide some stretch goals.

7. **Don't make statements that are inconsistent with the written review.** If a comment belongs in the discussion, it probably belongs in the written review. If you choose to give an employee a break by not recording a concern, at least tell the employee that "this time" you don't think it needs to be documented because you have come to an understanding that this event should not occur again. Let them know if the problem recurs you will document that the situation has not changed. If that happens, document that, after prior oral warnings, the concern has recurred. Be aware, however, that if the problem continues, your undocumented discussion will have less value in court than it would have had if you documented the incident at the time of the occurrence.

8. **Don't provide the written review without an explanation.** Your employee deserves to hear your assessment of her performance from you personally. Discuss the review with the employee without assuming she understands everything you've written. The purpose of the discussion is to create understanding and buy-in for next year's goals.

9. **Don't avoid or discount the employee's input or explanation of concerns.** You may not agree with an employee's rebuttal, but hear the employee out. Mutual respect is integral to an effective manager-employee relationship. You can disagree with the employee's explanation while you acknowledge

their perspective but still explain the reasons for your conclusions.

10. **Don't use casual idioms.** If you use a phrase that has a double meaning or has a literal meaning that is different from your intent, your words might not only cause misunderstanding, but they could incriminate you. If you say "I'll kill you if you don't stop doing that!" you know you don't mean what you say, but it wouldn't help your case if you are called on to defend your words. Words like *sweetie*, *honey*, or *darling* may have a fun or friendly intent, but can be taken as a sexual innuendo.

"DOS" TO PROTECT YOURSELF LEGALLY WHEN PRESENTING PERFORMANCE REVIEWS

Okay, now you know what not to do. Here are six things we recommend you do that can keep you from having regrets later in a courtroom.

1. **Do document facts instead of conclusions.** Give concrete examples of the employee's performance and the impact of their performance in the review period. Avoid paraphrasing issues without providing supporting facts. For example, say, "Jon called me a micromanaging witch when I spoke to him about his error in an order," rather than, "Jon was angry." It is a fact that Jon called you those names. The idea that he was angry is a conclusion you reached. As Sergeant Joe Friday would say, "Just the facts, ma'am. Just the facts."

2. **Do play devil's advocate with yourself.** Challenge your assessments to make certain you applied standards consistently when rating employees. Ask yourself if you are judging Maria's deficiencies in an area similarly to Jose's deficiencies in that same area. Ask yourself if your best employee had the same infraction or issues, if you would rate him the same way in that area. If you give an overall rating of "needs improvement" to an employee who scored higher in the individual categories than an employee who received an overall rating of "meets expectations," you're sending mixed messages to the employee. If employment decisions are made based on the review, there could be legal problems.

3. **Do take plenty of time to prepare and present the evaluation.** If you only spend five minutes reviewing your employee's work for an entire year, it signals to your employee that her work did not mean much to you. Take the time to review the employee's performance in detail. Set aside sufficient uninterrupted time to prepare to make it a meaningful review.

4. **Do give the employee opportunity for self-review and for comment right on the form.** Ask the employee to review his own performance prior to the formal review, and have a section on the form that indicates whether the employee agrees or disagrees with the review. Allow room for additional comments the employee may choose to make and a place on the form for the employee's signature. A signature on the form does not indicate that the employee agrees with your review, but his

signature does indicate that he has read and discussed it.

Employee self-evaluation can be effective in legal defense, because it can confirm the employee's duties and performance. The employee's signature that the review was discussed can be an important factor in a legal defense. It is difficult for an employee to claim that she didn't know how bad the situation was when the conversations were documented on the form.

5. **Do create a written plan to correct serious performance concerns.** If there are serious performance concerns, include an objective, measurable plan for improvement, with specific deadlines for implementation. Spell out consequences if the improvement plan is not fulfilled. In a court of law, a documented improvement plan establishes the existence of serious concerns and indicates a good faith effort to help the employee improve. That tends to negate accusations that a supervisor had unfair or discriminatory motives when disciplining or counseling an employee regarding performance.

6. **Do have a Human Resources representative (or other manager) read the written review before you review it with the employee.** Have an HR representative or other manager who is trained to recognize legal issues read your review to catch what you miss. Also, have another management representative in the room with you for the review, particularly where there are serious performance concerns.

WHAT THEY SAY ABOUT A "STITCH IN TIME" IS RIGHT

Following the above dos and don'ts can make the difference between a positive review that is legally defensible and a destructive review that could result in problems if challenged. Follow these dos and don'ts for the stitches in time that could save nine. The nine stitches you will save are tedious stitches that could cost a manager and organization time, stress, and money.

Preparation

SECTION II

Preparation

6

Documentation Dos and Don'ts

Once Burned, Twice Shy

Barbara was rushing to a meeting when she overheard one of her customer service representatives, Bill, hang up on a customer. She immediately made some quick notes about what she heard, dropped them into the working file she kept on Bill, and went on to her meeting. The next morning she reviewed her notes before calling Bill in to discuss what she observed. Bill had forgotten the incident but was reminded when Barbara described what she observed in detail. She and Bill explored alternative ways to handle customers like the one Bill hung up on. Once their meeting was complete, Barbara wrote notes to document the conversation and added these notes to Bill's working file.

Barbara wasn't always so thorough. She once had an employee who repeatedly got angry with customers. She would speak to him at her first opportunity each time and warned him that if he repeated his behavior, his job was at risk. When his behavior did not improve, Barbara drew up the papers to fire him. However, HR informed her that because she had no

documentation of the discussions, coaching, or ultimatum
she gave to him to correct his behavior, there were no grounds
to fire him.

As a result, Barbara had to start documenting his perfor-
mance problems and wait to terminate him until she had
built a sufficient file to substantiate her claims. In the mean-
time, he alienated several customers while Barbara built
the file.

WHAT EVERY MANAGER NEEDS
TO KNOW ABOUT PERFORMANCE
TRACKING SYSTEMS AND FORMS

"Document, document, document" is a familiar phrase
to most managers, but few managers know when, what,
and how to document. The hardest part of documentation is getting started. When you have a system of performance documentation in place, you'll discover it actually
saves you time, energy, and confusion. This chapter tells
you everything you need to know to get your system
going.

Your Main Performance Documentation
Tool: The Working File

What It Is

The working file replaces your memory of what your employees do or don't do. Record everything noteworthy,
with specific information about time, date, and details
of their activities. Always give the employee immediate
feedback and record specific details of those conversations.

Possible Formats

Your working file can be manila folders containing a performance log for each employee, or it can be a file for each direct-report employee created in a word processing program like Microsoft Word or a file for each direct report in an information management system like Microsoft Outlook. Your working file could be as simple as a notebook separated into sections with a different direct-report employee's name heading each section. If you use the computer or notebook approach, create a file folder to hold items such as letters of complaint, commendation, probation documents, and signed reviews.

Subfiles

Whatever format your working file takes, create two sub-files entitled "Employee Goals" and "Employee Notes."

Reminders

Create a task in Outlook, Palm, or other calendars with a reminder to enter information into your working file in case you forget. Even if you only enter information once a week, by the end of the year you will have fifty-two items in each working file providing dates and details for everyone's performance review. Your preparedness will make your performance reviews the most thorough reviews with the most on-target feedback that most employees will experience in their lifetime. Reminders will help you develop the habit of using your working file.

How Long to Keep

Working file notes are kept in your active files only as long as needed. If you made a note about poor performance and coached the employee and they changed their behavior, move the documentation into your storage files in case you need it in the future.

Transfer records of continued poor performance to a progressive discipline form, and transfer the working file notes to storage files.

Once performance review information is entered onto the performance review form, the information is officially communicated to the employee and has become a part of the personnel file; all of the notes in the working file to support that performance review are archived.

What to Include

Include specific behaviors and actions in your working file documentation.

Record both positive and negative behavior to:

- Let the employee know specifically what they did wrong or right, so they know what to change or do more of.
- Help you to logically consider any reasons for disciplinary procedures or for recognition and reward.
- Help yourself and your employee remember specific examples of exemplary or problem behavior.
- Give you the information you need to help employees succeed on the job.

Record any progress an employee made toward new goals, behaviors, or performance requirements in your performance log. Document all efforts the employee makes to improve themselves.

Personnel File

The personnel file is the official file kept on each employee of the company. It contains all of the employment documents such as insurance beneficiaries, emergency contact information, the job description, and the job application. It contains all official signed annual or semiannual performance reviews. It also contains all of the official signed and dated progressive discipline forms used during progressive discipline sessions.

This file is available to a manager or supervisor on a need-to-know basis. It can be made available to the employee by request in the presence of an official HR or senior staff member. Nothing should ever be removed or added to a personnel file without employee knowledge.

Performance Review Form

The performance review form is normally developed by the HR department of a company. It is personalized by the managers and supervisors with information from the goals and performance sections of the working file. Once this form is completed, shown, and discussed with the employee, it becomes an official performance review. The performance review form is the property of the company and stays in the personnel file as an official record.

Progressive Discipline Form

The progressive discipline form is designed by the HR department and is used when an employee has been unsuccessfully coached about their performance. It contains information that comes directly from the employee working file. Once this form is completed and presented verbally to the employee in the presence of an official witness, it becomes a part of their record. It is the property of the company and stays in the personnel file as an official record.

Before Putting Pen to Paper, Know Your Documentation Dos and Don'ts

Here are some tips to keep in mind before you put anything into writing.

DO	DON'T
Describe behaviors	Use labels (such as "sloppy")
Be specific	Be general
Document observed behavior	Use hearsay
Keep working files on everyone	Keep working files selectively
Document immediately	Create files retroactively
Document behavior	Document personality

THE DIFFERENCE BETWEEN OBJECTIVE AND SUBJECTIVE PERFORMANCE DOCUMENTATION

Objective observations are about tangible and measurable behavior. Subjective observations are a manager's opinions or interpretations of that behavior. You know you are being objective when your employee cannot argue with what you say. While an employee might argue that he does not do sloppy work, or that he really is a team player, he will find it more difficult to argue about the number of errors in a report or incidences of specific urgent phone calls that went unreturned to team members. Stick to concrete facts to stay on solid ground so the employee is forced to confront his own behavior.

PROPER DOCUMENTATION CAN FREE YOU FROM LEGAL BLUNDERS

To give great reviews, you need great documentation. To avoid legal blunders, you need great documentation. Observe the documentation dos and don'ts and refer to chapter 5 for more legal considerations in performance review documentation.

Janelle's One-Minute Documentation Process

Below is an easy-to-use documentation process for poor performance, good performance, and coaching. This form is intended to be quick and immediate. Right after an incident, quickly write down specific details. You don't need to say, "He said ... She said ..." It only takes a couple of sentences to summarize an occurrence. You don't have to keep these notes secret. If employees know what information you are recording it can be an important motivator for them to change.

ONE-MINUTE DOCUMENTATION FORM

Employee Name:

Date and Time:

Exemplary or problematic behavior:

Manager action:

Employee response:

Comments:

Documentation Example: Poor Performance
ONE-MINUTE DOCUMENTATION FORM

Employee Name: *Chris Smith*

Date and Time: *Monday, August 6, 2012—12:00 Noon*

Exemplary or problematic behavior: *Chris did not have last week's report on my desk by 10:00 a.m. as agreed.*

Manager action: *I asked him about it at 11:00 a.m.*

Employee response: *Chris said an emergency had come up with a computer problem. He got me the report at 12:00.*

Comments: *9/5/2012: Subsequent reports have been on time.*

Documentation Example: Excellent Performance
ONE-MINUTE DOCUMENTATION FORM

Employee Name: *Jan St. John*

Date and Time: *Tuesday, August 7, 2012—3:00 p.m.*

Exemplary or problematic behavior: *John Alexander, Director of Marketing, called me to compliment Jan's work on the design of the new report form.*

Manager action: *I told Jan what John said and thanked her for the good work.*

Employee response: *Jan said she was pleased and told me about how challenging it was to design a form that met everyone's needs.*

Comments: *9/13/2012: Art Billings mentioned how much he liked the new form.*

Documentation Example: Coaching
ONE-MINUTE DOCUMENTATION FORM

Employee Name: *Sarah Clemens*

Date and Time: *Friday, August 10, 2012—2:30 p.m.*

Exemplary or problematic behavior: *I found three errors on Sarah's spreadsheet for software receivables.*

Manager action: *I showed Sarah how to double-check her numbers to make sure they are accurate.*

Employee response: *She said she understood and would double-check every time now.*

Comments: *9/4/2012: Subsequent reports have been error-free.*

7

Setting the Scene
for Success

Privacy Please

I was presenting a seminar in a Holiday Inn one day, when I became curious about a man holding meetings in the lobby. He met with one woman when I started the seminar. He was talking to a different woman when I took my first break. He was talking to yet another woman when we broke for lunch. I walked within earshot and overheard the woman speaking defensively about how she was just trying to do her job. Suddenly it dawned on me . . . that man was conducting performance reviews in the lobby of the Holiday Inn. I wondered if the woman's defensiveness was aggravated by the public place she was being reviewed in. It can't have helped.

THE IMPORTANCE OF SETTING

The setting can make or break a performance review. Choose your location with as much care as you choose your words. Consider the feng shui of open communication and ease in integrated performance reviews.

Feng shui is the Oriental art of creating a space where the energy flows in a positive way. Feng shui can be very esoteric, but it also contains commonsense suggestions for the use of space and setting to establish the right tone for a meeting. Here are six setting tips to adjust your environment to support your objective in the performance review.

Setting Tip #1: Privacy

It is inappropriate for anyone else to be privy to a performance review discussion between a manager and her employee. Privacy needs to be both visual and auditory. Conduct the review in a place where no one will be looking in and guessing how it is going. Choose a place where no one will be able to hear. Lack of privacy can create anxiety and overreaction.

Setting Tip #2: Seating

Make sure chairs are comfortable and placed to keep you at the same level. It is awkward if one person is seated at a higher level than the other. Know where you want the employee to sit, and be sure the chair doesn't have papers on it when the employee arrives. If possible, avoid having a desk between you and your employee. A desk can create an uncomfortable barrier. You create a more open dynamic when you sit without a barrier.

Setting Tip #3: Orderliness

If your office is messy, straighten it before the review. Even if you are comfortable in a messy office, your employee may not be. Clutter can create distractions and take focus away from the employee. Feng shui regards clutter in the environment as a reflection of the state of mind. An uncluttered office is a fundamental principle of feng shui that adds to the coherence of everything that takes place in it.

Setting Tip #4: Lighting

Good lighting can enliven the interaction, while inadequate lighting can diminish the focus. Be certain that neither the employee nor you are in a shadow or darkened area. Obviously you will want to avoid lighting that is harsh.

Setting Tip #5: Placement

There is comfort, whether conscious or not, in having an escape route. Allow the employee that comfort by seating them closer to the door than you are. This is especially important if the review is being held in your office.

Setting Tip #6: Interruptions

Eliminate interruptions. Let your phone (both desk and cell phone) go to voice mail. Turn your pager off. Put a privacy note on the door, and give the employee your full attention.

MY PLACE OR YOURS? FURTHER LOCATION CONSIDERATIONS

Your office is the best location to hold a review if you can accommodate the setting tips. You tend to have the most control of your own space. If your office is not available, a private conference room can work. The employee's office is also an option if it is private and uncluttered.

If it is necessary to conduct a performance review off site, look for a place that accommodates the setting tips. Possibilities include hotel meeting rooms and outside conference rooms. Public places such as restaurants, coffee shops, and hotel lobbies do not have the privacy that reviews require.

8

Employee Preparation

A Performance Review Do-Over with Employee Preparation

Kate came to the seminar spitting mad. When the topic of the seminar turned to performance reviews, she was primed and ready to tell us about how she had been wronged. It was the day after her performance review, and the review she received was not the review she expected. She told the group about everything she had done in the previous year that her manager overlooked. She also told the group how she had a shout-out with her manager over his ratings. Kate knew that wouldn't help her case, but she felt powerless and unable to control her fury.

As the seminar progressed, the lightbulbs went on for Kate, and she realized she could have prevented the disastrous review she received. Her manager was busy and unaware of her day-to-day performance. He was only aware of her performance when the inevitable problems of working in a changing world surfaced. It was up to Kate to make her manager aware of her contributions.

Kate went home that night and prepared a summary of what she had accomplished in the previous year. The next morning she asked to share what she had formulated the night before. In addition to her accomplishments, Kate also listed areas that needed improvement and what she was doing to develop those areas. We laughed when we saw anger management on that list.

The next day Kate went in to apologize to her manager and ask for a do-over. Her manager felt bad about the situation as well and gladly responded to her constructive attempts to turn the situation around.

PREPARING THE EMPLOYEE FOR THE PERFORMANCE REVIEW

Employee preparation is essential to the success of a review. As an employee, you need to be an active participant in your own review. As a manager, it's important to guide your employees to prepare for their reviews.

Use the Performance Review Employee Checklist below for your own review, and provide it to your employees to help them prepare for their reviews. Create your own version of the employee preparation form to use in your own reviews and to help your employees fully participate in their reviews.

Performance Review Employee Checklist

This checklist is an important tool to make your performance review a complete success. It is worth your time to spend one to two hours reviewing your performance in the past performance period and establish ways we can work together to optimize your position. While your input is important to us, it's particularly important to you. It's your job and your life, so please take the time to make this a powerful experience.

1. PAST PERFORMANCE

❑ How have your job and responsibilities changed since your last review?

❑ What skills or areas have you grown or improved in?

❑ What lessons have you learned over the past year?

❑ How well did you meet your goals and objectives over the past year? Compare the past year with previous reviews. Be specific.

❑ What areas can you improve your performance in? And what activities/plan would assure that improvement?

2. PRESENT SITUATION

❑ What are the predominant current requirements of your job?

❑ What areas of challenge do you currently face?

❑ What do you enjoy about your job?

❑ Where does your job fit in the organization? (How does your job impact internal and external customers?)

❑ How happy are your customers with your performance?

3. FUTURE
- ☐ How will your job responsibilities stay the same or change in the future?
- ☐ List your job goals/objectives for the next six to twelve months.
- ☐ What areas do you need to grow or improve in to meet your goals?
- ☐ What training programs or coaching areas, if any, do you need to meet these goals?
- ☐ What additional assistance do you need to reach your peak performance level?
- ☐ What are your career goals?
- ☐ How can management help you be more effective?

STEPS FOR A MANAGER TO PREPARE THE EMPLOYEE

A manager's attitude toward reviews affects the attitude of employees. If the manager announces the review with trepidation, the employee will dread it. If the manager announces the review with confidence, the employee will look forward to it . . . or at least she will be more likely to look forward to it. Below are four steps for a manager to announce the review in a way that sets the tone and expectations that will lead to a productive performance review.

1. Set expectation for participation.
   Explain that the performance review meeting is meant to be a two-way conversation. Say,

- It's time to schedule our performance reviews. I am looking forward to our performance review discussion because it will give us the opportunity to have a joint planning session.

2. **Set the purpose and goal of the meeting.**
   Explain the purpose of the performance review. Tell him,

   - The review is an important opportunity for us to reflect on last year and plan together for next year.

3. **Provide a copy of the Performance Review Employee Checklist.**
   Give the employee a copy of the checklist and ask her to fill it out. Say,

   - This checklist will help us both to focus on the relevant events of last year. I'd like you to complete it and get it back to me one week before the review.

4. **Set a time for the review well in advance.**
   After you've set expectations and purpose, select a time that works for both of you and gives you both sufficient time to prepare. In most cases you'll want two weeks to prepare for the appointment. Say,

   - I'd like to meet at (time) on (date). Does that fit into your schedule and allow you enough time to prepare?

The more the manager and the employee prepare for the meeting, the more satisfying and productive the result will be. The manager doesn't have to work quite so hard, the employee is assured that his input is recognized, and both find themselves working as a team.

9

Manager Preparation

There is much more to performance reviews than showing up the day of the review. There are eleven simple steps to prepare for your review. Don't let the number of steps scare you. The few moments it takes to follow these steps will pay huge dividends in the long run.

STEP 1: SET THE APPOINTMENT WITH THE EMPLOYEE WELL IN ADVANCE AT A TIME CONVENIENT TO YOU BOTH. Give the employee at least two weeks to prepare for their review.

STEP 2: MAKE PREPARATION RECOMMENDATIONS TO THE EMPLOYEE. Refer to chapter 8 for recommendations of how employees can be active participants in their own reviews.

STEP 3: REVIEW THE EMPLOYEE'S JOB DESCRIPTION. Review employee job descriptions to be sure you are evaluating the employee based on relevant criteria. Also check the three Rs: does the job description *really reflect reality* now? If job requirements have changed, note that in the review.

STEP 4: REVIEW PERFORMANCE STANDARDS AND GOALS FOR THE EMPLOYEE. Review the criteria by which you will assess the employee, and note the criteria in a worksheet based on the one below. Note which job responsibilities are more important to effectiveness.

STEP 5: READ THE PREVIOUS REVIEW IN DETAIL. Read the review from the previous year to put this year's review in perspective and to note progress. Note goals and areas to improve.

STEP 6: REVIEW EMPLOYEE PERFORMANCE DATA. Review the monthly or quarterly interim reviews given during the year and your notes in your employee's working file. Enter your summary in a worksheet based on the sample below.

STEP 7: RATE PERFORMANCE BY COMPARING PERFORMANCE WITH GOALS AND STANDARDS. Determine if the employee met, did not meet, or exceeded expectations in each goal or area of responsibility.

STEP 8: SUPPORT EVERY CONCLUSION WITH DATA AND/OR EXAMPLES. List information on your worksheet to support every conclusion you draw, including the exceeds-performance areas.

STEP 9: SELECT PHRASES. Refer to the phrases in section IV and find the phrases that most accurately describe performance. Enter those phrases in your worksheet.

STEP 10: ADAPT THE PHRASES. Adapt phrases to your own style and to your employee's style.

STEP 11: FINALIZE PHRASES. Finalize phrases by reviewing chapter 10 to understand the seven motivators and adjusting the phrases to the particular situation.

DOS AND DON'TS OF SCRIPTING PHRASES

DO	DON'T
Decide what you want to say first, and then refer to phrases to determine how you want to say it.	Use a phrase that does not accurately describe performance.
Adapt phrases to your own style and situation.	Use a phrase that doesn't sound like you.
Determine supporting documentation for every phrase.	Use a phrase that you cannot support with examples.

SUCCESSFUL USE OF PHRASES

Scripted phrases are intended to help you effectively describe performance in an accurate way that motivates and enhances performance. They are intended to enhance genuine communication, not replace it. They are intended to summarize conclusions from observation, interim reviews, and documentation, rather than substitute for them. Phrases are to be used, not abused.

MANAGER PREPARATION WORKSHEET

Use the following worksheet as a model to create your own template worksheet.

Worksheet for Using Scripted Phrases During Performance Reviews

Employee's Name:

Position:

PERFORMANCE CRITERIA #1

Performance data

Specific examples

Criteria vs. performance comparison

Rating

Phrase (page from book)

Supplemental phrase

PERFORMANCE CRITERIA #2

Performance data

Specific examples

Criteria vs. performance comparison

Rating

Phrase (page from book)

Supplemental phrase

SAMPLE MANAGER
PREPARATION WORKSHEET

The following is an example of a completed worksheet.

Worksheet for Using Scripted Phrases
During Performance Reviews

Employee's Name: Michelle Swanson

Position: Sales Representative

PERFORMANCE CRITERIA #1: Sell $1,000,000 worth of widgets in a year.

Performance data: Michelle sold $920,000 of product.

Specific examples: 4 months were below $80,000 (June $60,500, July $59,300, August $61,000, and December $65,000)

Criteria vs. performance comparison: Criteria is a minimum of $80,000 per month. Performance was a total of $74,200 short of the annual goal.

Rating: Below performance standards

Phrase (reference from book page 110): "Overpromises and underdelivers."

Adapted Phrase: "You committed to your quota of $1,000,000, but did not deliver on it."

Supplemental phrase: "Makes excuses for errors. Needs to focus more on own responsibility for mistakes made."

Adapted Phrase: "When I spoke to you at the end of each month about not reaching your goal, you blamed shipping, the weather, and the customers. You need to focus on what you can do to overcome any challenges to meet your goals."

CONCERNS ABOUT AUTHENTICITY

Some managers are concerned about sounding phony when they use phrases from a list. This is a legitimate concern but not a problem if you carefully select your phrases to accurately reflect the situation and if you adapt them to your own style. Select phrases that reflect what you would have said on your own if only you had thought of it, and no one will be able to accuse you of being phony.

10
Motivate Employees to Change

What motivates your employee? When you understand the answer to this question, you'll know how to phrase your points and where to place the focus of your interaction. There are seven motivators that will enhance the power of your review when appropriately applied.

MOTIVATOR #1: RECOGNITION

Everyone likes to hear what a good job they are doing, but some people are especially motivated by praise. It is common that people in support positions, helping jobs, and sales are highly motivated by acknowledgment. When you use acknowledgment as a motivator, be sure to make it specific:

- I really appreciate that you got the project done on time and under budget.

- You were stellar at bringing a diverse team together to reach the goal quickly.
- The fact that you brought in that new customer with our new product line sets you up as a role model to our other reps.

MOTIVATOR #2: TANGIBLE REWARDS

Recognition is one type of reward for work well done, but some employees like more tangible rewards. The most common rewards associated with performance reviews are raises. Other motivating rewards are time off, a closer parking spot, and a corner office. Associate the reward with the specific accomplishments that justify the reward.

Sample phrases are:

- Because your sales have consistently been 20 percent above quota, you will receive a bonus and your name on a parking spot for a year.
- You led your team to completing each project on time and on budget for the past year. Congratulations. That's why we are giving you a bonus and the part-time assistant you requested.

MOTIVATOR #3: ACCOMPLISHMENT

People who thrive on accomplishment love challenge. They need goals that stretch their knowledge and skills. They are motivated by the thought that they are doing what no one else can do and what no one has done before.

To motivate someone who gets high on accomplishment, say things like:

- **You began the year as a new member of our team, and what a year it's been! If we had a Rookie of the Year Award, you'd win for surpassing your goal. Congratulations!**
- **Because you've grown so much, I have two goal recommendations that I think you'll find challenging. I recommend we set a goal for you to develop your project management skills and another one for you to take a lead role in our new product launch.**

Ask questions that inspire those who are motivated by accomplishment, such as:

- **How can you benefit from completing this task?**
- **How will it feel when it is done?**
- **What is the end result of your work?**

MOTIVATOR #4: ALTRUISM

Many employees are motivated by altruism and the belief that they are contributing to a noble cause. Altruism in the workplace can include helping others, coaching or teaching them, making their job easier, or helping out when others are sick or new to the team. Altruism in the workplace also can include a sense of contributing to the greater good through the mission of the organization. To motivate an employee by altruism, talk about the impact on others when you assign a new task or ask for a behavior change.

- When you are late, your colleagues have to work overtime and may miss personal appointments.
- We need for you to be 100 percent accurate on these specifications because it could cause an injury to someone if you're not.
- Since you know the process so well and you are such a good teacher, I'd like you to show Mark how to use it.
- Streamlining this process will make a huge difference to patient care.

MOTIVATOR #5: BELONGING

People get a sense of security and identity from being included in a group. Working together for a common goal creates bonding that fosters meaning in work and life. People who are very motivated by "belonging" do very well on teams. You can use this as either a positive or negative motivator.

- Because you have proven your ability in this area, I will put you on the interdepartmental team to design a plan for the whole company.
- Your teammates have lost trust in you because you did not follow through on your responsibility. I will have to take you off the team until you can prove you will meet your deadlines.

MOTIVATOR #6: FEAR

Everyone is motivated by fear in one way or another. Some might fear missing a deadline, and others might fear losing a job. Some employees are sensitive to fear, and others have higher thresholds for fear. A sensitive employee might respond to the hint of a problem, but a less sensitive employee needs concrete warnings to take you seriously. Point out what the employee will lose if they don't change their behavior. For example:

- **If you continue this behavior, you will be put on probation.**
- **You will lose your rights to park in the building if you don't go by the rules.**
- **You will no longer be a part of the team if you miss another deadline.**

MOTIVATOR #7: CONTROL

Some people find it important to be able to control their work environment. Control ranges from how they do their job, to the hours they work, to having input into decisions that affect them. Some people want to do their job their way. You may hear them say, "Just tell me what the goal is, and I'll figure out how to make it happen." They get their thrill out of the mental challenge of figuring out the solution. To capitalize on their control needs, you can use approaches like:

- **We need to streamline the packaging process. I think you can cut the time it takes by at least 25 percent. Go for it!**

- **Because you have proven your self-discipline while working from home one day a week, I will expand that to two days a week now.**

Choose the motivator that best inspires each person, and choose your phrases accordingly.

11

Learn from Pros and Amateurs: Performance Review Tales of Triumph and Terror

Performance reviews are among the most powerful tools in a manager's toolbox. Properly done, the power of performance reviews is constructive. Improperly done, the power of performance reviews is destructive. You don't have to take our word for it. We have stories from employees and managers that illustrate the impact of reviews better than our words ever could. These stories give you the opportunity to learn from the experiences of others.

EMPLOYEES TALK ABOUT REVIEWS THEY RECEIVED

The Power of Collaboration

Told from the perspective of an employee, this story illustrates the value of involving employees in the review process.

We just started having formal reviews in my organization this year. I was a bit nervous about my review, but my nervousness dissipated when my boss asked for my input in preparing for his own review. He showed me what he had prepared so far, and I told him about things I thought should be included. It was a real exchange of trust, and it created a foundation that carried over into my review. When he gave me my review, he said, "Your review is no different from everything else we do: it's a team effort."

I feel so supported by my boss, and we trust each other more than ever—happy me!

The Destructive Power of Not Listening

This story illustrates how destructive a review can be when a manager overfocuses on a single issue and does so without inviting feedback.

Over thirteen years ago I received a review that was so unfair that I still cringe when I remember it.

My boss told me, "An employee overheard you on the phone earlier this week on a personal call. We are paying you far too much money to make personal calls from work. That is why you are given a lunch hour, and we expect all personal calls to be made on your own time." I was given no opportunity to explain that I was making a local call to my dentist for my stepdaughter, who was in agony with a toothache. At no time had I been told there were to be absolutely no personal calls, even to make an emergency appointment for a sick child. I was stunned at the unfairness and also stunned that after a year of doing a good job, this topic dominated my review.

That was the beginning of the end of my employment there. I love where I work now, but that memory still affects me emotionally.

The Power of Employee Preparation

The following story demonstrates how employee preparation for a review can add to fairness, accuracy, and goodwill. In this story, the employee initiated their involvement. Many employees won't think to initiate involvement, so don't leave the responsibility for inclusion to the employee.

For several years my performance reviews have been less than stellar. I always got the annual increment, but the reviews were laden with remarks about my style and my perceived lack of commitment to the organization. I would be called into the review meeting without much notice and handed the written review to read while the supervisor waited for me to finish. Many things on the review took me by surprise, and I was unprepared to react and discuss the comments in a reasonable manner.

Finally, I asked that the written review be given to me at least one day in advance so I could read, digest, and prepare for the review meeting. By having time to get ready, I was much more prepared to calmly discuss the issues in question. In fact, several things were removed from the review after our meeting. I must be doing something right, because I had my annual performance review last week, and it was a complete success.

The Power of Praise with Particulars

A performance review that shows an employee their manager cares can be a memorable and even life-changing event, as the following letter indicates.

Ann and Barb, my closest friends and coworkers, and I were due for our annual performance reviews. Situated low on the hierarchical totem pole—administrative clerk typist B (one step higher than clerk typist A)—we didn't think much about it. Our supervisor, Peg Hindman, on the other hand, did.

Typically, as defined by the state system and as demonstrated by other section supervisors, each section supervisor was required to complete a one-page, written evaluation for each employee in their section and share the results with the employee in a thirty- to forty-minute meeting.

Not Peg. Peg voluntarily revised the standard evaluation form, distributed blank copies to everyone in her section, and asked us to fill it out so we could participate in a two-way conversation at the review meeting!

As I hurried to complete my copy of the review, I noticed Peg working at her desk to complete each of ours. I felt surprised by the time she took to pause, reflect, gather supporting information, and carefully jot notes regarding everyone's performance for the past year.

During my review, which lasted nearly an hour and a half, Peg described various situations in which I had excelled or added value to our section. She even invited her immediate supervisor to sit in and give additional comments. (Wow, this was big!)

At the end of my review, Peg smiled and handed me an envelope with a letter inside. "Robin, this is a letter of recommendation. You are far more capable than what this position, admin. clerk typist B, allows, and I do not want to see you working in this section a year from now."

When Ann, Barb, and I gathered for our afternoon break, each of us could hardly wait to share the news of our exceptional reviews. Near the end of our excited conversation, I asked with some embarrassment, "Did either of you get . . . a letter?" Ann and Barb exchanged glances, "Yeah. You, too?"

My elation ebbed—"Oh . . . it's probably a form letter . . ."—and quickly surged, as each of us read ours aloud. The letters were as extraordinary as the reviews—each one elegantly pointing out our unique talents and contributions.

Within the year, Ann, Barb, and I—as Peg suggested—moved on. Ann was promoted to supervisor, and Barb and I went back to school. Several years later, I cofounded a consulting and training business, Ann became the statewide coordinator for university donations, and Barb was named associate registrar.

(I still have my letter.)

MANAGERS TELL THEIR TALES

The One-Minute Performance Review Travesty

The following are the actual words of a manager at a performance review:

> *"Well, your performance is pretty much the same as last year. You're doing just fine. You get the standard cost-of-living raise of 3 percent. Sign here."*

This manager wondered why her consistently good performer left and went to the competition for the same pay. We think the way she conducted her performance reviews played a part.

The Manager's Reward

Employees are not the only ones who find well-done reviews rewarding. Managers reap rewards as well, as the following story illustrates.

> *Over the years I experienced my fair share of performance reviews as a staff person—most of them were either a waste of time or torturous. When I was promoted to a manager position, I was determined to make the review a positive and powerful experience for both my staff and myself. Because I had no good role models, I read several books about delivering performance reviews. I was amazed at the amount of prework all of the authors advocated, but I decided to try it. I had to create a discipline in myself of writing notes on my staff's positive and negative behaviors. It was not easy at first. After awhile, it just became second nature. When it came time for the actual*

reviews and I reread all of the notes, I was able to see trends in behavior that gave me insights into the outcomes of my staff's performance. I could better understand the "why" of their performance. When we had the performance review meeting, I really felt I was their coach preparing them for the next season. It was one of the most rewarding experiences I've had as a new manager.

Dealing with the Tough Stuff

Often managers avoid addressing poor performance with people who are emotional or intimidating. If the negative performance is not dealt with and the employee continues to get away with it, the employee thinks the behavior is fine. This is the confession of one of those managers and how he handled the situation.

Bill and I shared a delightful sense of satisfaction at the first performance review I gave him. We both smiled ear to ear when I told him I rated him acceptable in communication with the phrase: "Makes his points clearly, kindly, and directly," and exceptional in teamwork with the phrase: "Brings out the best in the team." Just a month ago, that could not have happened.

A month before, we were headed for a train wreck. I was tempted to ignore the problems. I would tell myself that I was too busy, but the truth was, I was intimidated. Performance reviews were less than a month away, and I knew I couldn't wait to talk to Bill about the problems the team had with him. It was only fair to talk in time for him to make changes before the performance review. Plus it was only fair to the team for me to handle the problem right away.

I always viewed myself as a nice guy. I want my team to get along and for them to enjoy working for me. I hired Bill because I needed an additional team member and interviewed people from within the company. Bill interviewed well, had fine reviews from his previous manager, and appeared to be a great fit. However, it wasn't long before Bill started to intimidate others on the team in order to get his way. He would get loud and sarcastic when driving his point home. The other team members were upset and almost spent more time complaining to each other about Bill than doing their work.

I'm more of a soft-spoken person and did not relish the idea of having to talk to Bill about his intimidating behavior, for fear he'd use it on me. I got some help from HR.

My HR representative said she'd be glad to be in the meeting with me, and she provided me with some excellent guidance. She advised me that intimidation is often a sign of insecurity. So we laid out a discussion that balanced Bill's positive performance with the discussion of the intimidation. We put the discussion in the context of fitting in, belonging on this team, and truly being persuasive. We talked about the negative impact his loud voice and sarcasm had on getting the acceptance and buy-in of his teammates to his ideas. I used specific instances to illustrate it. I told him I wanted to help him fit in and be successful here. I told him I wanted to work with him to get his performance up before his performance review.

I was pleasantly surprised with Bill's response as we made our points. He said he had never felt like he had anyone in his corner before. He always had to fight to get heard. He asked for some guidance in how to make his points differently, because he was used to having to "shout it out."

By looking at the situation from what motivates Bill, I was able to present touchy information in a sincere way that he appreciated. He and I had a new respect for each other after that.

That meeting changed everything, and I've never enjoyed a performance review as much as the one I gave Bill one month later. We felt like we had really accomplished something, and I learned how important it is to address issues before a performance review.

The High Impact of Performance Reviews

Most people remember their performance reviews. We're sure you have stories about reviews you have given or received . . . and your employees have stories they could tell about reviews you have given. Reviews provide an opportunity to make a difference in people's lives. Be sure the difference your reviews make is positive.

Perfect Words
Are Not Enough

12

Body Language Dos and Don'ts

An Unintended Message

Janice had no idea that she intimidated her employees by crossing her arms and sporting a stern expression. She was surprised when an employee openly told her, "I feel intimidated." Janice's real attitude was interest, but her body communicated severity. From that moment on, Janice consciously kept an open body posture and a more relaxed, friendly expression when she was listening to her staff. Janice's management skills improved tremendously that day when she discovered how she came across and decided to do something about it.

It doesn't matter how good your words are . . . if your body language undermines your words. This chapter will tell you what body language to avoid or embrace in performance reviews.

WHY BODY LANGUAGE IS PARTICULARLY IMPORTANT IN PERFORMANCE REVIEWS

Because performance reviews affect people personally, because they relate to people's self-image, and because they can impact employees' careers, you need to be particularly conscious of your body language in your performance reviews. A gesture that is innocent in another context could send a signal that creates defensiveness, undercuts your words, or causes you to lose credibility in the performance review. For example, ordinarily if you cross your arms or put your hands on your hips, people don't think too much about it. During a performance review these same gestures might speak so loudly your employee can't hear a word you say.

WHAT YOU WANT YOUR BODY TO SAY

You want your body to communicate a balance of authority and confidence. Your body needs to communicate that you are the leader who can help the employee achieve their goals. You want your demeanor to be serious without being threatening. To do this, avoid passive gestures and expressions that weaken your position of authority and avoid aggressive expressions and gestures that intimidate.

BODY LANGUAGE TO FAVOR AND AVOID
DURING THE REVIEW

FAVOR	AVOID
Arms: Open, relaxed arms, hands, and gestures.	**Arms:** Crossed arms.
Hands: Purposeful handling of documents and open gestures.	**Hands:** Clenched fist, pointing finger, covering your mouth, and fidgeting.
Handling Documents: Occasional reference to documents as needed.	**Handling Documents:** Focusing more on documents than the employee.
Eye Contact: Meet eyes for several seconds and look away. Be sensitive to their comfort level of eye contact.	**Eye Contact:** Being at a different eye level by standing while the employee sits, staring, and averted eye contact.
Facial Expression: A neutral, friendly face that communicates pleasant seriousness and interest.	**Facial Expression:** Excessive smiling, scowling, furrowed brow.
Personal Space: Sitting between two to four feet from the employee.	**Personal Space:** Sitting closer than two feet away, sitting more than four feet away, and hiding behind a desk.

Body language is so important that it is essential to make sure yours is saying what you want it to say. The best kind of feedback on your body language is to see it for yourself by watching a videotape. Like Janice, mentioned earlier, there is much to be gained from feedback from others.

VOICE TONE

A slight change in voice tone can make the world of difference in meaning. For instance, the following sentence can have the opposite meaning, depending on where you put the vocal emphasis: "You have made some improvement."

It's also important to not let your personal emotional reactions or judgments come through in your tone. Many times we are unconscious of how we sound, so it could be helpful to record yourself or seek feedback from a peer. The following are some tips to favor or avoid:

VOCAL TONES TO FAVOR AND AVOID
DURING THE REVIEW

FAVOR	AVOID
A calm, neutral tone of voice as if you were asking someone to pass the butter.	Sarcastic, edgy tone.
A variance of modulation.	Constantly ending remarks in an upswing.

FAVOR	AVOID
Conversational volume.	Speaking more loudly or softly than needed for understanding.

You can change body language and vocal habits that don't serve you into habits that enhance and support the message you want to send.

13

Role-Play Your Way to Performance Review Effectiveness

Practice Makes Permanent

No matter how accurate John's reviews were, there were a couple of employees who knew how to work him and get him to change the review on the spot.

Jeanne did it with tears. She sniffed as she complained about how any issues were not her fault and how she really was doing the best she could and how if she didn't get a higher rating she wouldn't get the raise she needed to pay her daughter's tuition.

Ron worked John with subtle anger. He accused John of favoring the female employees, and John wondered . . . was Ron hinting that he might make it difficult for John if the rating was not changed? He wasn't quite sure, but he felt an impulse to "go along to get along."

John was so uncomfortable with both situations that he gave in against his better judgment. That is, until he started role-playing before the reviews.

John and another manager got together to practice their re-

views. They knew each other's direct reports, so they practiced as if they were them. John had prepared his partner with possible employee responses. His colleague practiced those responses, even exaggerating them sometimes. John practiced staying calm and firm while the other manager role-played a tearful and an angry response. When they were done, John's colleague gave him feedback on the things John did that worked and what John needed to do to be more effective. After that practice session, John was amazed at how smoothly things went . . . and by how many of the problems that commonly occurred did not come up at all because John was not contributing to an unhealthy dynamic.

PRACTICE IN ADVANCE

The time to practice a new behavior is before it really matters. The mere idea of a performance review can trigger a panicked reaction in both managers and employees. That's why role play before a review can be a powerful tool. It gives you a chance to practice interacting in a thoughtful and responsive manner rather than a reactive way, in an environment that is safe and that provides feedback.

To role-play, use the five steps below:

Step 1: Anticipate Everything

Since John had been challenged by Jeanne and Ron in performance reviews in the past, he knew exactly what kind of responses to prepare for. However, even if you have never given a review before, if you know yourself and your employees, you can anticipate the kinds of challenges you are likely to face. Some employees may resist your constructive feedback, and others may get defensive about anything that is less than stellar. There is no excuse for failing to prepare for behavior that is predictable. Review the ten manager misconceptions in chapter 1 to avoid any of them.

Step 2: Find an Appropriate Practice Partner

Not everyone is a good candidate for a role-play partner. Look for someone whom you trust enough to share your own limitations, as well as those of your staff. For example, if discussing how you felt manipulated by Jeanne might cause someone you're considering as a role-play partner to think less of her or of you, or if you are afraid your admissions would become a hot topic around the water cooler, choose someone else. Choose someone who can help you work with difficult traits rather than judge them. It helps if the person you pick has some acting ability and doesn't mind pushing the envelope with you.

Step 3: Prepare Yourself and Your Partner

Tell your partner about the behavior styles of the person whose review you are going to practice. Fill them in on the kinds of roadblocks you have experienced with this person in the past, and ask them to simulate the worst-case scenario.

Step 4: Practice

Pretend your practice partner is your employee, and run through the review process from the first notification to your parting words. Have your partner play the employee role of the most challenging scenario. For the more difficult segments, try several ways to handle the situation to see which one works the best.

Step 5: Debrief

Get feedback from your colleague on how you did. Evaluate the worst and best things you did, and get suggestions for the best way to handle the conversation or situation. Practice areas that were weak until they become flawless.

PRACTICE MAKES PERMANENT

The more you practice, the more successful your review will be. It's easy to slip into thinking you are prepared once you have the forms filled out and the appointment set. The most powerful preparation is to perform a dry run. Your confidence and comfort will be communicated during the review.

14

Standards
of Responsible
Communication

From Unsupportive to Supportive

Judy seemed very pleasant, so I was surprised when she told me her employees used to leave her office in tears. She had no understanding of why, until someone explained that her all-business manner was intimidating. After learning that, Judy developed a practice of making at least one pleasant personalized comment in every interaction. Judy was amazed at what a difference a personal comment made in her rapport and effectiveness.

From Sarcastic to Respectful

For Rodney, it was the elimination of sarcasm that turned his performance as manager around. He made a commitment at a seminar to eliminate the use of sarcasm with his employees, and although it took several months for employees to feel safe around him, they eventually dropped their defensiveness and opened up with him.

From Vague to Specific

Bernice discovered that she needed to be more specific. She used to tell employees they needed to improve in certain areas like quality, but failed to give them concrete examples of what they were doing wrong and what they needed to do instead. They would leave her office knowing their work was unacceptable but not knowing how to improve. That changed when Bernice started giving more concrete examples of what they were doing incorrectly and examples of exactly what correct performance was. If they needed it, Bernice would coach them in how to make the change.

Each of the managers described above discovered that they needed to set standards of communication for themselves, with specific action steps to meet those standards. Judy's new standard was to be friendly, Rodney's was to be civil, and Bernice's was clarity. Standards are norms for responsible and effective communication. Making the extra effort to establish and follow standards can make the difference between an unsuccessful and a successful performance review.

SIX COMMUNICATION STANDARDS FOR EFFECTIVE PERFORMANCE REVIEWS

Below are six communication standards that apply specifically to the performance review.

Standard #1: Supportive

Be on his team

Adversarial communication derails performance reviews. Reviews are a "we" process, not a "me-against-you" process. Be sure your tone and words communicate that you are there to support the employee, not to play a game of gotcha. A great way to be supportive is to emphasize solutions when discussing performance challenges.

FAVOR	AVOID
We'll make a plan to bring you up to standards.	You figure it out.
I'll help you address this.	Don't ask me. It's your job.
Let's find an approach that will work.	I told you that wouldn't work.
You need to apply yourself more by . . .	You don't apply yourself.

Standard #2: Individualized

Target your words to each employee

Because each employee is unique, your words in the review need to reflect their individual performance. While your review forms might require you to evaluate performance in terms of categories, be sure your words relate to your employees as individuals. Avoid labels that put your employees in boxes. For example, I was once told that I was low-maintenance, while some of my coworkers were high-maintenance. Even though I came out on the winning end of the labeling, it felt odd to know we were all put in one of two boxes.

FAVOR	AVOID
It's great how you manage to get team members to understand each other.	You're one of our team players.
Your performance on the widget appraisal shows you know how to make things happen.	We've pegged you in the shaker and mover group.

Standard #3: Respectful

Honor your employee

Speak respectfully to your employee, even if they are not speaking respectfully to you. Avoid exaggeration, sarcasm, threats, and yelling.

FAVOR	AVOID
We need to work on your cooperation with other team members by . . .	You are part of a team, in case you didn't notice.
You have three incidents of coming in late. That means you will be suspended if you are late again.	You're never on time.
If this problem isn't solved, the result will be . . .	Get your act together or else.

Standard #4: Objective

Address the problem, not the person

When you share conclusions and ratings with your employees, support every subjective remark with an objective example or by data. For example, if you tell your employee they have improved in immediacy of communication, give examples to substantiate it.

FAVOR	AVOID
I have noticed over ten occasions where you were unable to read your own handwriting.	You're sloppy.
You closed some deals I didn't think anyone could nail.	You're amazing.
Your marketing campaign did not increase sales.	You don't have a clue about marketing.
I need your work delivered on time.	You're lazy.

Standard #5: Consistent

Give ongoing feedback

If there is anything in the review that would surprise the employee, leave it out. Surprises in reviews indicate that you didn't do your homework. Surprises should never occur. The information in the review needs to be consistent with what you have been telling the employee all along.

FAVOR	AVOID
As we discussed in our interim review . . .	I've been meaning to tell you . . .
We already established that . . .	I assume you know that you . . .

Standard #6: Specific

Be concrete by supporting conclusions with examples

Use exacting words that present a precise picture of employee performance and your expectations. Choose words that clarify any ambiguity.

FAVOR	AVOID
Your sales need to increase by 20 percent.	Do better.
You often negate ideas at meetings before the presenter has finished explaining.	You have a bad attitude.
Your thirty-second response time average was a major achievement.	Great job.

IMPLEMENTING THE STANDARDS

While all the communication standards are important, your best approach in implementing them is to decide which ones you need to work most on, and make an absolute commitment to them. The phrases in this book are designed in compliance with responsible communication standards.

Great Phrases for Powerful Performance Reviews

15

Interpersonal and Team Skills

The phrases in this chapter will help you describe performance regarding interpersonal and team skills. These phrases are the summary phrases to be used in step 3 of the five steps of the masterful performance review that is detailed in chapter 3 and outlined below.

Step 1: Greet the employee
Step 2: Set expectations
Step 3: Summarize performance
    Strengths
      1. Summary phrase
      2. Documentation/example phrase
      3. Impact phrase
      4. Action phrase
    Areas that need improvement
      1. Summary phrase
      2. Documentation/example phrase
      3. Impact phrase
      4. Action phrase
      5. Gain agreement

Step 4: Look forward
Step 5: Close

EXCEPTIONAL VERSUS ACCEPTABLE

We combine the *exceptional* and *acceptable* phrases because the difference between exceptional and acceptable performance is usually a matter of frequency and degree. Adapt the phrases to your situation with adjectives that indicate the frequency and degree you see in the characteristics you are rating.

BONUS SUPERLATIVES

Each category has a bonus phrase for those employees whose performance surpasses the ordinary. We call them *bonus superlative phrases.* These phrases are fun and rewarding to an employee whose performance almost defies description. If you've ever read the negative performance phrases that circulate the Internet (for example, has delusions of adequacy), bonus superlative phrases are our attempt to counteract those and provide a light, humorous way to acknowledge exceptional actions.

DEVELOPMENT PLAN

Substantiate each summary phrase with a documentation/example phrase to provide the explanation for your rating and phrase selection. Then use an action phrase to suggest ways for improvement. In this resource, we provide an action phrase for each summary phrase in the "Needs Improvement" section. We offer these to encourage emphasis on what you want rather than what you don't want when addressing performance problems.

ADAPTABILITY

Exceptional/Acceptable

- Sees change as opportunity.
- Switches gears when needed.
- Knows when to hold them and knows when to fold them.
- Presents new ideas to address problems.
- Is willing to try new approaches.
- Adapts to new policies and procedures.
- Adapts to changing deadlines.
- Willing to accept new assignments.

Bonus Superlative Phrase

- Halfway there before others begin.

Needs Improvement

- First response to change is why it won't work. Needs to consider positives of changes.
- Has a difficult time switching gears. Needs to develop a way to bring a task to immediate closure when called on to shift focus.
- Clings to obsolete procedures. Needs to update skills in the area of . . .
- Clings to old priorities. Needs to reevaluate priorities from moment to moment.

- Resists trying new approaches. Needs to stay open to new ways of doing things.
- Does not adapt well to changing deadlines. Needs to learn to reevaluate priorities.

ACCOUNTABILITY/RELIABILITY

Exceptional/Acceptable

- Does what he says.
- Takes responsibility for errors.
- Sees projects and responsibilities through to completion.
- Meets deadlines.
- Says what she means. Can be taken at her word.
- Is always prepared.

Bonus Superlative Phrase

- More reliable than death, taxes, and Old Faithful.

Needs Improvement

- Overpromises and underdelivers. Needs to be more realistic in promises made.
- Makes excuses for errors. Needs to focus more on own responsibility for mistakes made.
- Has incomplete projects. Needs to carry projects through to completion.
- Misses deadlines. Needs to budget buffer time to guarantee completion of projects.
- Hedges answers and requires probing to get a straight answer. Needs to practice straightforwardness.

- Can be unprepared. Needs to create checklists to ensure preparation.

APPROACHABILITY

Exceptional/Acceptable

- Is easy to talk to.
- Welcomes questions.
- Invites input.
- Is available when needed.
- His door is open enough that coworkers get what they need, but not so open that he doesn't get the work done.
- Creates a sense of safety and welcome for others.
- Inspires an open-communication culture.
- Makes people feel at home.

Bonus Superlative Phrase

- She couldn't be more approachable even if she wore a welcome sign.

Needs Improvement

- Difficult to speak to. Needs to set other considerations aside and give others his full attention.
- Appears to resent questions. Needs to consider helping team members as part of her job.
- Does not welcome input. Needs to listen to what someone has to say before drawing conclusions.
- Hard to reach. Needs to check messages at least three times daily.

- Approachable to a degree that allows others to inter-fere with his meeting deadlines. Needs to create un-interrupted times for himself.
- It feels risky to approach her. Needs to be more open to contact.
- Coworkers go around him in an attempt to avoid conflict. Needs to listen to others' concerns without reacting to encourage team members to keep him in the loop.
- Makes people feel unwelcome. Needs to create a welcoming environment.

ATTITUDE
Exceptional/Acceptable

- Looks for reasons and ways for projects and ideas to succeed.
- Is enthusiastic about work and projects.
- Likes to contribute.
- Puts team interests ahead of her individual inter-ests.
- Cooperates with team members.
- Is solution-focused, rather than focused on pinning blame.
- Makes lemon coolers out of lemons.
- Is realistically positive.
- Looks to optimize every situation.

Bonus Superlative Phrase

- His ability to look on the bright side of any situation is illuminating.

Needs Improvement

- Overly focused on problems, limitations, and why things won't work. Needs to consider possibilities and search for solutions.
- Lacks enthusiasm about work and projects. Needs to find ways to enjoy her work or find other work that she can be enthusiastic about.
- Seems unconcerned with contributing. Needs to take ownership of team needs.
- Puts personal interests ahead of team needs. Needs to recognize that personal interests are ultimately served by team interests.
- Does not cooperate with team members. While dissenting input is welcome during discussion, he needs to defer to group consensus once it is reached.
- Stays focused on what doesn't work. Needs to think of what can be done about existing situations.
- His attitude is positive but not realistic. Needs to develop positive realism.
- Does not see the opportunity in situations. Needs to look to optimize every situation.
- Approaches task with an "I can't" attitude. Needs to focus on what she can do.

COMMUNICATION: VERBAL

Exceptional/Acceptable

- Speaks clearly and is easy to understand.
- Makes points in a clear, concise manner.
- Adapts to the communication style of the listener.
- Is focused and targeted in conversation.

- Speaks positively.
- Clearly communicates expectations.
- Contributes to creating clarity in group discussions.
- Initiates difficult conversations.
- Speaks in a way that encourages and opens discussions.
- Keeps stakeholders informed about information that affects them.
- Speaks to the technical understanding of listeners.
- Knows the difference between passiveness, aggression, and assertiveness and chooses assertiveness.
- Asks thoughtful, effective questions.
- Has an effective vocal tone.
- Asks questions when clarification is needed.
- Speaks to build consensus.
- Is willing to say "I don't know."
- Speaks to calm people who are upset.

Bonus Superlative Phrase

- He could inspire Donald Trump to be quiet and listen.

Needs Improvement

- Speaks in a way that is difficult to follow. Needs to determine and organize key points before speaking.
- Rambles. Needs to streamline messages.
- Speaks the same way to everyone regardless of style. Needs to consider the communication style of the listener.
- Goes off on tangents. Needs to stay focused.
- Is discouraging due to overfocus on problems and negatives. Needs to communicate more possibilities and positives.

- Hints when communicating expectations. Needs to communicate expectations clearly.
- Allows misunderstandings to fester without addressing them. Needs to initiate difficult conversations at the first sign of misunderstanding.
- Can be critical of others' ideas, thereby shutting down conversations. Needs to reinforce input by others.
- Does not keep stakeholders informed about issues that affect them. Needs to anticipate who needs to be informed and keep them in the loop.
- Does not simplify messages to increase the understanding of the listener. Needs to determine the technical level of whomever she is speaking to.
- Comes across as passive-aggressive. Needs to be clear and direct without slipping into aggression.
- Asks questions in a way that sounds threatening or critical. Needs to assure that questions are intended for clarification, not challenge or judgment.
- Speaks in a monotone (aggressive tone, overly excited tone). Needs to speak in a modulated tone.
- Improvises instead of asking questions when instructions are unclear. Needs to ask clarifying questions to assure understanding.
- Speaks in a divisive way. Needs to build consensus by focusing more on areas of agreement before addressing his own opinions.
- Misleads others by pretending to know things she does not. Needs to say "I don't know."

COMMUNICATION: WRITTEN

Exceptional/Acceptable

- Written communication is error-free.
- Written communication is catchy, interesting, and easy to understand.
- Writing is persuasive and effective.
- Writes winning proposals.
- Writing is clear, concise, and well-organized.
- Makes complex ideas understandable.
- Writes in an easy-to-read, conversational style.
- Displays understanding of the principles of effective writing.
- Introduces points, elaborates points, and summarizes points for clarity.
- Develops points in a clear, understandable way.
- Documents points well for clarity and credibility.

Bonus Superlative Phrase

- Writes so well that even a procedures manual he wrote would be a page-turner.

Needs Improvement

- Written communication has an unacceptable number of errors. Needs to use spell-check and review writing before submission.
- Written communication style is dry and overly complex. Needs to simplify and personalize.
- Writing is clinical and unconvincing. Needs to address the needs of the reader.
- Proposals do not persuade. Needs to talk more in terms of benefits.

- Writing is unclear, poorly organized, and lengthy. Needs to outline writing and reduce word count by one-third in editing.
- Makes simple ideas complex. Needs to target a lower level of understanding and communicate details on a need-to-know basis.
- Writing is excessively formal. Needs to imagine being in conversation when writing.
- Violates many principles of effective writing. Needs to take a class or otherwise study effective writing.
- Makes points without clarification. Needs to introduce points, elaborate on points, and summarize points for clarity.
- Makes points randomly and often does not develop them. Needs to present points systematically.
- Does not document points well for clarity and credibility. Needs to ensure that every point has data or an example for documentation.

CONFLICT MANAGEMENT
Exceptional/Acceptable

- Communicates directly, respectfully, positively, and specifically in conflict.
- Addresses issues as they arise.
- Is as strong as he needs to be and no stronger.
- Sounds calm in addressing conflict.
- Listens well to others, even when she does not agree with what the others are saying.
- Eliminates blame in discussing conflict.
- Pinpoints the source of conflict and addresses it.

- Can disagree without offending.
- Stays focused on a positive outcome, even when angry.
- Works cooperatively to resolve conflict.
- Can accept criticism calmly.

Bonus Superlative Phrase

- Could bring peace to the Middle East.

Needs Improvement

- Communicates indirectly and vaguely in conflict. Needs to be more direct and specific.
- Allows issues to fester in conflict. Needs to address issues as they arise.
- Initially minimizes issues, and then swings into overreaction. Needs to be as strong as required and no stronger.
- Gets agitated when addressing conflict. Needs to stay calm and speak in a calm tone.
- Tunes the other person out and stops listening when conflict arises. Needs to listen well to others, even when he does not agree with what the others are saying.
- Quick to blame in addressing conflict, which incites defensiveness. Needs to avoid blame in discussing conflict.
- Battles symptoms and does not address the source of conflict. Needs to address the source of conflict.
- Disagrees in a way that creates defensiveness. Needs to allow other people to save face by disagreeing without ridiculing ideas she objects to.

- Loses perspective of the possibility of resolution in conflict. Needs to stay focused on a positive outcome, even when angry.
- Attempts to resolve conflict on his own without involving the person he is having conflict with. Needs to work cooperatively to resolve conflict.
- Does not accept or respond well to criticism. Needs to consider and respond to criticism calmly and openly.

CONTRIBUTES TO TEAM GOALS
Exceptional/Acceptable

- Holds team goals clearly in mind.
- Will place team goals ahead of personal goals.
- Pitches in to team efforts where needed.
- Refers to team goals in planning sessions and conversations.
- Keeps focused on team goals, even when diversions abound.
- Understands her contribution and carries her weight.

Bonus Superlative Phrase

- Brings home the whole pig, not just the bacon.

Needs Improvement

- Appears unaware of and not focused on team goals. Needs to prioritize according to team goals.
- Will place personal goals ahead of team goals. Needs to realize that personal goals are enhanced by contributing to team goals.

- Does not take ownership of team needs. Too limited by job description. Needs to pitch in to team effort where needed.
- Does not refer to team goals. Needs to refer to team goals in planning sessions.
- Does not carry his weight. Needs to be accountable for obligations in meeting team goals.

COOPERATION AND TEAMWORK

Exceptional/Acceptable

- Sees what needs to be done and does it.
- Shares expertise freely.
- Works effectively with others.
- Asks others how she can help.
- Is a valuable asset to brainstorming sessions and idea development.
- Brings out the best in the team.
- His teams work well.
- Helps other succeed whenever possible.
- Inspires others to cooperate.
- Contributes to team discussions.

Bonus Superlative Phrase

- If the Chicago Cubs had her on the team, they would win the World Series.

Needs Improvement

- Does not recognize needs of other team members. Needs to notice what needs to be done and pitch in.

- Guards expertise. Needs to share expertise more freely.
- Does not work effectively with others. Needs to seek and consider others' input.
- Does not offer to help others. Needs to offer support to others.
- His feedback during brainstorming sessions interrupts the flow. Needs to acknowledge others' ideas to keep the process moving.
- She has a divisive impact on the team. Needs to consider impact of comments on the team as a whole.
- His teams do not work well. Needs to work to create a collaborative team dynamic.
- Focuses on own advancement to the exclusion of the advancement of others. Needs to help others succeed whenever possible.
- Speaks in a way that divides teams. Needs to avoid gossip and inspire others to cooperate.
- Withholds ideas in team discussions. Needs to freely share ideas with the team.

CREATIVITY

Exceptional/Acceptable

- Comes up with original ideas to solve problems and enhance business.
- Questions common procedures for improved methodology.
- Finds a way to make things work when standard procedure doesn't.

- Finds ways to improve operations.
- Contributes new ideas to discussions.
- Develops creative ideas that have practical applications.
- Sees what is, imagines what could be, and asks why not.
- Finds creative solutions for problems that satisfy everyone.
- She doesn't just figure out new ways to cut the pie. She figures out how to make the pie bigger.

Bonus Superlative Phrase

- Leonardo da Vinci would envy him.

Needs Improvement

- Gives up on solving problems when old solutions don't work. Needs to invent original ideas to solve problems and enhance business.
- Takes common procedures as mandates and does not improve on them. Needs to question common procedures to improve methodology.
- Rarely questions the status quo. Needs to find ways to improve operations.
- Does not add ideas to discussions. Needs to contribute new ideas, even if she is not certain of their viability.
- Develops creative ideas but fails to apply them to practical application. Needs to consider the applicability of ideas and work to implement them.
- Is limited by what is and does not seek alternatives. Needs to think in terms of "what if."

- Does not consider alternative solutions to meet more people's needs. Needs to look for creative solutions to satisfy everyone.

DIVERSITY/INCLUSIVENESS

Exceptional/Acceptable

- Treats different demographic groups equally.
- Sees diversity as a valuable organizational strategy.
- Supports organizational workforce initiatives.
- Treats all ethnic groups with respect.
- Respects different ideas.
- Bridges the gaps between different demographic groups.

Bonus Superlative Phrase

- Finds common ground in polar opposites.

Needs Improvement

- Shows preferential treatment to some groups over others. Needs to treat different demographic groups equally.
- Does not recognize the strategic value of diversity. Needs to recognize diversity as a valuable organizational strategy.
- Makes decisions that are not in line with organizational workforce initiatives. Needs to support organizational workforce initiatives.
- Tells ethnic jokes. Needs to treat all ethnic groups with respect.
- Attempts to impose own cultural view. Needs to respect different ideas.

- Takes sides when there are issues between different groups. Needs to help groups bridge the gaps.

INITIATIVE
Exceptional/Acceptable
- Sees what needs to be done and does it.
- Requires minimal supervision.
- Takes a leadership role when appropriate and needed.
- Seeks out and recognizes new opportunities.
- Takes charge in the absence of instructions.
- Does things without needing to be told.
- Anticipates and prepares for problems.
- Willingly tries new procedures.
- Creates opportunities for himself.
- Takes responsibility for her own career development.
- Is always prepared.
- Takes a bad situation and makes it good . . . Takes a good situation and makes it great.

Bonus Superlative Phrase
- He does not just predict the future; he invents it.

Needs Improvement
- Ignores things that need to be done. Needs to be more aware of needs and meet them.
- Requires excessive supervision. Needs to listen more carefully to directions and expectations and to self-manage.
- Does not step in when there is a void in leadership. Needs to take a leadership role when appropriate and needed.

- Does not recognize or capitalize on new opportunities. Needs to seek out opportunities.
- Waits for direction in the absence of instructions. Needs to take charge when instructions are not available.
- Does not take action unless told. Needs to observe what is needed and do things without being told.
- Plans for the best-case scenario without creating a backup plan for problems. Needs to anticipate and prepare for problems.
- Resists new procedures. Needs to develop willingness to adjust to procedures as they change.
- Expects the organization to find opportunities for her. Needs to create opportunities for herself.
- Expects the organization to be responsible for his advancement. Needs to take responsibility for his own career development.
- Gets caught unprepared. Needs to anticipate problems and prepare for them.
- When faced with a difficult situation, she does not look for possibilities. Needs to look for ways to make a bad situation good and a good situation great.

LISTENING
Exceptional/Acceptable

- Pays careful attention when spoken to.
- Responses make it clear he listened well.
- Acknowledges what was said before making her own point.
- Attempts to understand before attempting to be understood.

- Makes a point of clarifying anything she finds unclear.
- Maintains excellent eye contact when someone else is speaking.
- Makes a point of ensuring the speaker feels heard.
- Avoids distractions when someone is speaking.
- Follows directions well.
- Hears what is said the first time.
- Allows speaker to make his point uninterrupted.

Bonus Superlative Phrase

- Listens so well she can summarize what we say better than we can say it.

Needs Improvement

- Appears distracted when spoken to. Needs to pay more careful attention and maintain eye contact.
- Asks questions that indicate he was not listening. Needs to listen for understanding.
- Appears to be waiting for her turn to speak rather than listening. Needs to acknowledge what was said before making her own point.
- Seems more concerned with being heard than with understanding. Needs to attempt to understand before trying to make himself understood.
- Assumes she understands. Needs to question assumptions and clarify anything she is not sure of.
- Avoids eye contact. Needs to maintain eye contact when someone else is speaking.
- Responds to comments quickly without acknowledgment. Needs to ensure the speaker feels listened to by acknowledging what they say.

- Divides attention when listening. Needs to avoid distractions when someone is speaking.
- Makes errors in following directions. Needs to be more attentive to directions and to repeat them back to ensure understanding.
- Requires repetition. Needs to listen more carefully the first time, possibly taking notes to increase focus.
- Interrupts. Needs to allow speakers time to make their points.

PERSUASION

Exceptional/Acceptable

- Bases arguments on sound reasoning and convincing facts.
- Is aware of and speaks to others' true motivations.
- Easily dissolves rock-solid resistance in others.
- Brings others around to his point of view and even leaves them with the impression it was their idea.
- Handles arguments and objections skillfully.
- Uses diplomacy rather than power to persuade others.
- Addresses people where they are in their thinking and walks them step-by-step to where she wants them to be.
- Balances reason and emotion in persuasion.
- Can persuade without opposing.

Bonus Superlative Phrase

- Can talk the birds out of the trees and even get them to sing harmony.

Needs Improvement

- Does not elicit support for ideas effectively. Needs to speak to the needs of others.
- Does not back up assertions with adequate data. Needs to base arguments on sound reasoning and convincing facts.
- Does not speak to individual motivations. Needs to become aware of what motivates others and speak to it.
- Attempts to coerce team members into compliance rather than to dissolve resistance. Needs to see the points of others' resistance as her opportunity to persuade them and to address their specific concerns.
- Attempts to persuade create resistance. Needs to attempt to persuade others based on understanding.
- Insists on being right at the expense of being persuasive. Needs to refrain from focusing on getting credit and acknowledgment, and strategically agree with others.
- Appears threatened by arguments and objections. Needs to permit others to express their objections to understand how to bring them around to his way of thinking.
- Attempts to persuade others without a clear understanding of their perspective. Needs to meet people where they are in their thinking and walk them step-by-step to where she wants them to be.
- Ignores the emotional component in persuasion efforts. Needs to balance reason and emotion in persuasion.

- Relies too heavily on the emotional component in persuasion efforts. Needs to balance reason and emotion in persuasion.
- Attempts to persuade with pressure. Needs to replace intimidation tactics with motivation techniques.

PUNCTUALITY
Exceptional/Acceptable

- We can set our watches by him.
- Can be counted on to be on time.
- Carries through on time commitments.
- Sets realistic deadlines and meets them.
- Understands that being on time is a significant part of her job responsibility.
- Knows the importance of timeliness in everything he does.

Bonus Superlative Phrase

- She never lets deadlines die.

Needs Improvement

- Not punctual. She is consistently a minimum of ten minutes late, keeping coworkers, managers, and even customers waiting. Needs to allow extra travel time to assure timeliness.
- We cannot be certain that he will be on time. Needs to regard time commitments as binding.
- Does what she says she will, but often is late to deliver. Needs to consider promises more carefully before making them.

- Misses deadlines due to overobligation and inability to negotiate timelines. Needs to assess priorities and negotiate timeline changes when necessary.
- Sets unrealistic deadlines he does not meet. Needs to evaluate deadlines realistically to increase punctuality.
- Does not appear to understand that being on time is a significant part of her job responsibility. Needs to do whatever it takes to be on time.
- Seems unaware of the importance of deadlines. Needs to understand the impact of timeliness in everything he does.

16

Management and Leadership Skills

The phrases in this chapter will help you describe performance regarding management and leadership skills. These phrases are the summary phrases to be used in Step 3 of the five steps of performance review mastery detailed in chapter 3 and summarized in the beginning of chapter 15, page 107. Please review these pages to understand the context these phrases are intended to be used in before proceeding. The beginning of chapter 15 also explains the use of exceptional versus acceptable phrases, bonus superlatives, and the use of phrases to create a development plan.

ADMINISTRATIVE SKILLS

Exceptional/Acceptable

- He creates systems to streamline department procedures.
- Keeps scrupulous records.
- Keeps files current and easy to access.
- Skilled in managing electronic files.

- Skillfully manages large quantities of information.
- Executes projects impeccably.
- Maintains seamless day-to-day functions.
- Makes the coordination of multiple events seem effortless.
- Keeps the office running seamlessly.
- Coordinates the uncoordinated.

Bonus Superlative Phrase
- Such an effective administrator, she could herd cats.

Needs Improvement
- Lacks an organized approach to regular tasks. Needs to create systems to streamline procedures.
- Records contain errors. Needs to focus on accuracy in maintaining records.
- Loses or takes an inordinate amount of time finding records. Needs to create a system to be able to locate records quickly.
- Files are not current and are difficult to access. Needs to redesign his filing system and file weekly.
- Loses files in the computer. Needs to redesign her electronic filing system.
- Becomes overwhelmed by large quantities of information. Needs to develop an information management system that helps him prioritize data.
- Overlooks details in project management. Needs to train in project management and implement a project management system.
- Inconsistent in keeping up with recurrent responsibilities. Needs to schedule time and reminders for routine day-to-day activities.

- Does not effectively coordinate office functions. Needs to develop systems to streamline operations.

COACHING SKILLS
Exceptional/Acceptable

- Sees the greatness in others and draws it out through coaching.
- Helps people dream big and take decisive action.
- Helps employees define their goals and create concrete steps to reach them.
- He can point out weaknesses in a way that builds strength.
- Inspires people to give their best effort.
- Provides information in palatable, bite-size, digestible nuggets.
- Shows people how to succeed but doesn't do it for them.
- Has insights that go to the core of the issue, not relying on the superficial symptoms.
- Provides employees with inspiration, awareness, and tools to excel.

Bonus Superlative Phrase

- If careers were like football teams, her coaching would lead many to the Super Bowl.

Needs Improvement

- Does not aid employees in developing their skills. Needs to draw out skills through coaching.
- Does not help employees see the big picture. Needs to help people dream big and take decisive action.

- Sets goals for employees without their input and without providing guidance as to how to reach these goals. Needs to help employees define their goals and create concrete steps to reach them.
- Focuses disproportionately on weaknesses in a way that demoralizes. Needs to focus on ways to build strength and motivation to improve.
- Creates resentment when coaching. Needs to inspire people to give their best effort by applying tailored motivational tools.
- Overloads employees with information. Needs to determine how much they can handle and provide information in palatable, bite-size, digestible nuggets.
- Spoon-feeds rather than allowing employees to draw their own conclusions. Needs to lead people to discover how to succeed, rather than do it for them.
- Provides employees with inspiration and awareness but not tools to excel. Needs to offer tools to achieve goals once he gets them pumped up.
- Does not inspire employees to go the extra mile. Needs to find what motivates employees to excel.

DECISION-MAKING SKILLS
Exceptional/Acceptable

- Carefully considers options before making decisions.
- Makes quick decisions under pressure.
- Bases decisions on long-term consequences.
- Solicits and considers stakeholder input before making decisions.

- Consults with subject experts prior to making decisions.
- Knows which decisions to make and which to delegate.
- Decides well under pressure.
- Unbiased in decision making.

Bonus Superlative Phrase

- Decides with the foresight of Noah, who made the decision to build the ark before it started raining.

Needs Improvement

- Does not consider all options before making decisions. Needs to be open to more alternatives.
- Loses focus under pressure. Needs to learn to stay calm in order to quickly make appropriate decisions under pressure.
- Sacrifices long-term consequences in favor of immediate benefits in making decisions. Needs to base decisions on long-term benefits.
- Does not involve stakeholders in decisions. Needs to solicit and consider stakeholder input before making decisions.
- Does not consult with subject experts prior to making decisions. Needs to determine who can best advise in situations requiring expertise and consult them.
- Makes decisions for employees that they are capable of making themselves. Needs to delegate decisions to empower employees and encourage autonomy.
- Makes decision before starting the decision-making process and then uses the decision-making process

to justify decisions that have been predetermined. Needs to stay open to where the evidence leads in decision making.

- Wastes time on insignificant decisions. Needs to allocate time invested in decisions based on the significance of the decision.

DELEGATION

Exceptional/Acceptable

- Uses delegation to develop employees.
- Uses delegation to pinpoint employee strengths.
- Maximizes her own productivity by delegating tasks that do not best use her skills.
- Gives clear explanations when he delegates.
- Picks the right task for the right employee.
- Avoids reverse delegation by providing clear instruction.
- Holds employees accountable for their delegated tasks.
- Communicates for buy-in by emphasizing importance of tasks in delegation.

Bonus Superlative Phrase

- Delegates better than Tom Sawyer.

Needs Improvement

- Hoards tasks with development potential. Needs to use delegation to develop employees.
- Dismisses employee potential without testing through delegation. Needs to use delegation to pinpoint employee strengths.

- Holds on to tasks that are best handled by someone else. Needs to maximize his own productivity by delegating tasks that do not best use his skills.
- Does not provide sufficient information or training when delegating. Needs to provide clear explanations and training when she delegates.
- Does not match tasks to employee skills and goals. Needs to consider employee skills and goals in delegation.
- Takes back projects at first sign of difficulty. Needs to avoid reverse delegation by providing clear instruction and guidance when necessary.
- Does not follow through on monitoring delegated tasks. Needs to hold employees accountable for their delegated tasks.

EMPLOYEE EVALUATION SKILLS
Exceptional/Acceptable

- Uses evaluations as a motivational tool.
- Uses evaluations as a developmental tool.
- Prepares well for appraisals.
- Conducts appraisals on time.
- Communicates importance of appraisals to staff.
- Conveys a positive attitude toward appraisals.
- Appraisals accurately reflect performance.
- Involves staff in reviews.
- Bases reviews on goals developed throughout the year.
- Avoids surprises at the review by communicating issues as they arise.

Bonus Superlative Phrase

- His reviews are more useful than the discovery of fire, more insightful than Confucius, and more fun than a trip to Disney.

Needs Improvement

- Evaluations are discouraging to employees. Needs to focus more on motivational coaching.
- Does not use evaluations to develop employees. Needs to set goals with employees.
- Attempts to conduct appraisals from memory without adequate preparation. Needs to invest a minimum of one hour per review to be better prepared.
- Conducts appraisals late or not at all. Needs to set a schedule and stick to it.
- Downplays importance of appraisals to staff. Needs to communicate their value.
- Conveys an attitude of dread toward appraisals. Needs to convey a positive attitude toward appraisals.
- Appraisals reflect personal preferences rather than accurately reflecting performance.
- Appraisals excessively reflect recent performance, rather than reflecting the entire performance period. Needs to use review to reflect the entire performance period.
- Does not involve staff in reviews. Needs to teach employees how to prepare for their own reviews and ask them questions during the review that invite them to participate.

- Does not track goals throughout the year. Needs to set and track goals to provide a foundation for the review.
- Will save discussion of performance issues until the review. Needs to communicate issues as they arise.

GIVING FEEDBACK
Exceptional/Acceptable

- Delivers feedback in an effective, constructive manner.
- Provides feedback to help others achieve success.
- Provides honest feedback in a way that facilitates improvement.
- Makes a point of offering positive feedback to reinforce desired behaviors in addition to providing negative feedback when needed.
- Feedback accurately reflects performance.
- Keeps personal agendas out of feedback.
- Feedback includes facts, impact, and suggestions.
- Times feedback effectively.
- Offers feedback immediately when appropriate.
- Praises in public, criticizes in private.

Bonus Superlative Phrase

- She can tell people what they're doing wrong and have them be grateful for the information.

Needs Improvement

- Delivers feedback in a divisive, ineffective manner. Needs to focus more on what it would take for success.

- Avoids offering difficult feedback even when employees need to hear it to improve. Needs to take a deep breath and speak up when needed.
- Feedback comes across as denunciation. Needs to provide honest feedback in a way that facilitates improvement.
- Downplays and whitewashes problems in feedback. Needs to provide honest feedback in a way that facilitates improvement.
- Only provides feedback when there are problems. Needs to make a point of offering positive feedback to reinforce desired behaviors in addition to providing negative feedback when needed.
- Feedback reflects personal biases. Feedback needs to more accurately reflect performance.
- Feedback lacks specific information. Feedback needs to include facts, impact, and suggestions.
- Does not offer feedback in a timely fashion. Needs to time feedback effectively.
- Withholds feedback until reviews. Needs to offer feedback immediately.

INITIATIVE
Exceptional/Acceptable
- Sees what needs to be done and does it.
- Solves problems as they arise.
- Does what needs to be done without being asked.
- Is a self-starter.
- Requires minimal supervision.
- Anticipates what is needed and prepares in advance.

- Recognizes and takes advantage of opportunities.
- Has original ideas that work.
- Springs into action as soon as the need arises.
- Consistently updates skills.
- Looks for new ways to apply his skills.

Bonus Superlative Phrase
- The management version of the big bang.

Needs Improvement
- Does not address problems until told. Needs to notice what needs to be done and do it.
- Waits to be told to solve problems. Needs to solve problems as they arise.
- Waits for direction. Needs to recognize needs and be a self-starter.
- Requires an excessive amount of supervision. Needs to work with more independence.
- Does not prepare or take action until absolutely necessary. Needs to anticipate what is needed and prepare.
- Misses opportunities. Needs to recognize and take advantage of opportunities.
- Does not look beyond what is presented. Needs to think originally.
- Only acts in reaction to outside pressure. Needs to spring into action as soon as needs arise and before she is forced to.
- Does not update skills unless initiated by management. Needs to take initiative in updating skills.
- Does not help management find uses for his skills. Needs to take responsibility for finding new ways and situations to apply his skills.

MEETING MANAGEMENT

Exceptional/Acceptable

- Creates and distributes agendas prior to meetings.
- Adheres to agenda during meetings.
- Maintains order in meetings.
- Keeps meetings on track.
- Skillfully handles interruptions and negative interactions.
- Successfully elicits input from all attendees.
- Effectively focuses meetings on outcome.
- Summarizes decisions with concrete action steps.
- Holds team accountable for implementing action steps from previous meetings.

Bonus Superlative Phrase

- Success means getting on her coveted meeting invitation A-list.

Needs Improvement

- Does not provide agendas or sufficient advance information for attendees to prepare for meetings.
- Does not keep meetings on track. Needs to adhere to agenda during meetings.
- Loses control in meetings. Needs to maintain order in meetings.
- Allows meetings to go off on tangents. Needs to keep meetings on track.
- Allows interruptions to hijack meetings. Needs to handle interruptions more skillfully.
- Allows a few attendees to dominate meetings. Needs to elicit input from all attendees.

- Meetings address issues without addressing solutions. Needs to effectively focus meetings on outcomes and solutions.
- Participants leave meetings without an understanding of what actions are expected as follow-up. Needs to summarize decisions with concrete action steps and allocated responsibilities.
- Does not follow up on action steps. Needs to hold people accountable for follow-through from previous meetings.

ORGANIZATION
Exceptional/Acceptable

- Maintains an orderly workspace.
- Turns chaos into order.
- Creates easy-to-follow work systems that successfully organize operations.
- Has a place for everything and everything is in its place.
- Skillfully manages multiple projects without losing track of any detail.
- Organizes workload according to priorities.
- Can find anything immediately.
- Organizes files so others can find them.
- If he can't find it, it never existed.

Bonus Superlative Phrase

- So organized that a needle trying to hide from her in a haystack doesn't stand a chance.

Needs Improvement

- Does not maintain an orderly workspace. Needs to put organization on his daily to-do list.
- Spends an unacceptable amount of time trying to find things. Needs to create orderly files.
- Approaches workload in a haphazard manner. Needs to create easy-to-follow work systems that successfully organize operations.
- Workspace is chaotic. Needs a place for everything and to keep everything in its place.
- Will get absorbed in one project to the exclusion of others. Needs to budget time for multiple projects without losing track of any detail.
- Does not do first things first. Needs to organize workloads according to priorities.
- Often takes an undue amount of time to locate items. Needs to develop an organizational system to find things more quickly.
- Organization works for her, but others can't find things. Needs to organize so others can find items.

PRIORITIZATION

Exceptional/Acceptable

- Has a keen sense of priorities.
- Puts first things first.
- Efficiently manages competing priorities.
- Knows what matters most.
- Knows which requests to honor and which requests to decline.
- Does not waste time on nonessential activities.
- Prioritizes activities based on long-term objectives.

- Eliminates activities that do not add value.
- Practices zero-sum prioritization.

Bonus Superlative Phrase

- Uses the Smokey the Bear system of business prioritization. She prevents (office) fires before they happen.

Needs Improvement

- Lacks a sense of priorities. Needs to chart importance and urgency of projects for daily, weekly, and monthly prioritizing.
- Will allow low-priority activities to take precedence over high-priority activities. Needs to develop and implement a system of prioritization that enables him to put first things first.
- Does not balance competing priorities. Needs to efficiently budget time for all priorities.
- Does not differentiate between high and low priorities. Needs to weigh consequences of projects to determine what matters most.
- Allows herself to be sidetracked by requests that lack priority. Needs to learn how to say no diplomatically.
- Spends time on nonessential activities at the expense of essential activities. Needs to recognize and eliminate nonessential activities.
- Planning considers short-term outcomes at the expense of long-term priorities. Needs to prioritize activities based on long-term objectives.
- Does not question low-value activities. Needs to eliminate activities that do not add value.

- Maintains low-value processes and procedures. Needs to practices zero-sum prioritization by setting priorities based on value rather than precedent.

STAFF DEVELOPMENT
Exceptional/Acceptable

- Provides training to develop weak and strong areas in employees.
- Shares expertise to develop employees.
- Encourages employee input and ideas.
- Encourages employee autonomy when appropriate.
- Rotates staff to develop job understanding.
- Walks in employee shoes to understand their needs and challenges.
- Encourages staff to develop knowledge and skills.
- Provides mentoring to staff.
- Created a mentoring program to develop staff.
- Keeps employees inspired by job enhancement.
- Systematically enhances job descriptions to expand employee skills and motivation.
- Aligns work assignments with employee goals.
- Delegates to develop employees.
- Uses mistakes as learning and development opportunities.

Bonus Superlative Phrase

- He could inspire and teach a pig to fly.

Needs Improvement

- Does not provide training. Needs to support staff to meet goals by providing training.

- Provides limited training to develop weak areas, but does not provide training to develop excellence in areas of competence. Needs to provide training to develop both weak and strong areas in employees.
- Routinely shoots down employee ideas. Needs to encourage, listen, and respond to employee input and ideas.
- Maintains excessive control of the front-line decisions. Needs to encourage employee autonomy when appropriate.
- Does not encourage cross-training. Needs to rotate staff to develop a broader department understanding.
- Lacks direct involvement in employee jobs. Needs to work alongside employees occasionally to provide input.
- Seems unwilling to adapt employee workload to accommodate employee development. Needs to allocate time for staff training.
- Misses opportunities to mentor staff. Needs to provide on-the-spot mentoring to staff.
- New employees lack needed guidance and orientation. Needs to create a mentoring program to develop new staff.
- Does not recognize that monotony reduces quality of work and motivation. Needs to keep employees inspired by job enhancement.
- Does not expand job descriptions to encourage employee growth. Needs to align job responsibilities with employee skills and interests.
- Guards own expertise around subordinates. Needs to share expertise to develop employees.

- Appears unaware of employee goals and does not help employees achieve them. Needs to align work assignments with employee goals.
- Holds on to interesting assignments and only delegates routine assignments. Needs to delegate to develop employees.
- Takes employee to task for mistakes without focus on what can be learned. Needs to use mistakes as learning and development opportunities.

SUPERVISORY

Exceptional/Acceptable

- Makes expectations clear.
- Conducts regular progress reviews.
- Addresses issues immediately.
- Holds employees accountable for meeting performance standards and goals.
- Is accessible to employees.
- Understands the demands of employee responsibilities.
- Pitches in when employees need support.
- Treats employees fairly.
- Divides work into clear and manageable pieces.
- Removes obstacles to employee goal achievement.
- Stays apprised of what happens in his department.
- Effectively handles employee differences and conflicts.
- Asserts authority appropriately and effectively.
- Maintains harmonious work environment.

Bonus Superlative Phrase

- Supervises with super-vision.

Needs Improvement

- Is unclear in expressing expectations. Needs to be specific about deadlines, desired outcome, and budget.
- Does not provide consistent feedback. Needs to conduct regular progress reviews.
- Does not address issues as they arise. Needs to address issues immediately.
- Is overly tolerant of poor performance. Needs to hold employees accountable for meeting performance standards and goals.
- Does not make adequate time for employees and can be difficult to reach. Needs to be accessible to employees.
- Overloads employees with unreasonable demands. Needs to gain a greater awareness of the demands of employee responsibilities.
- Will not make time to assist when subordinates are overloaded. Needs to pitch in when employees need support.
- Does not reward or punish the same behavior in all employees. Needs to treat employees fairly.
- Work assignments are unclear. Needs to divide work into clear and manageable pieces.
- Ignores obstacles to employee performance. Needs to uncover and remove barriers to employee goal achievement.

- Is unaware of the issues of day-to-day operations in her department. Needs to stay better apprised of departmental occurrences.
- Allows employee differences and conflicts to fester. Needs to quickly and effectively handle employee differences and conflicts.
- Comes across as heavy-handed. Needs to assert authority appropriately and effectively.
- Appears hesitant to express authority. Needs to assert authority appropriately and effectively.
- Ignores workplace disharmony. Needs to address issues to maintain harmonious work environment.

17

Task and Technical Skills

The phrases in this chapter will help you describe performance regarding task and technical skills. These phrases are the summary phrases to be used in Step 3 of the five steps of performance review mastery detailed in chapter 3 and summarized in the beginning of chapter 15, page 107. Please review these pages to understand the context these phrases are intended to be used in before proceeding. The beginning of chapter 15 also explains the use of exceptional versus acceptable phrases, bonus superlatives, and the use of phrases to create a development plan.

ACCURACY

Exceptional/Acceptable

- Understands why accuracy is essential.
- Meets exacting standards.
- Gives careful attention to detail.
- Extremely low error rate.

- Can be trusted to catch his own errors.
- Holds others to exacting standards.
- Keeps accurate records.
- Checks detail in depth.
- Documents operations in detail.
- Gets it right the first time.

Bonus Superlative Phrase

- The world clock is off by two milliseconds a century. This employee's accuracy puts the world clock to shame.

Needs Improvement

- Sacrifices accuracy for speed. Needs to understand why accuracy is essential and take the time to eliminate errors.
- Mistakes have cost money. Needs to be more exacting.
- Sends out work containing errors. Needs to review work for details before sending out.
- Unacceptably high error rate. Needs to recheck work before submitting.
- Does not catch her own errors. Needs to create systems to catch errors.
- Too lenient with errors others make. Needs to hold others to exacting standards.
- Records are not sufficiently detailed or accurate. Needs to keep detailed and accurate records.
- Does not confirm details. Needs to check detail in depth.
- Documentation lacks accuracy, depth, and detail. Needs to document in detail.

ANALYTICAL SKILLS

Exceptional/Acceptable

- Displays clear reasoning skills.
- Methodical in analyzing data and solving problems.
- Performs complex calculations with ease.
- Data analysis results in actionable conclusions.
- Comprehends complex data and issues and draws accurate conclusions.
- Develops deep and accurate insights from research.
- Maintains awareness of the big picture while accurately analyzing details.
- Objectively allows data to lead him to accurate conclusions.
- Stays focused on goals and objectives while analyzing relevant details.

Bonus Superlative Phrase

- Better than Sherlock Holmes.

Needs Improvement

- Often draws wrong conclusions from data. Needs to double-check conclusions against data.
- Does not perform complex analysis. Needs to develop skills in analyzing data and solving problems.
- Analysis sometimes overemphasizes unimportant details. Needs to put each piece of data in perspective, while performing complex calculations.
- Sometimes has paralysis by analysis. Data analysis needs to result in actionable conclusions in a reasonable time frame.

- Lacks a grasp on complex data. Needs to take more time to comprehend complicated data and issues to draw accurate conclusions.
- Gets lost in details and loses awareness of the big picture. Needs to synthesize the big picture and details while performing analysis.
- Uses the analytical process to lead her to a preconceived conclusion. Needs to objectively allow data to lead her to accurate conclusions.
- Goes on tangents that do not align with goals and objectives in analysis. Needs to stay focused on goals and objectives while analyzing relevant details.

CLERICAL AND SECRETARIAL

Exceptional/Acceptable

- Is one step ahead of those he supports.
- Anticipates and meets the needs of supervisors.
- She can keep the most chaotic and busy executive organized.
- Can lay him hands on records immediately.
- Uses cutting-edge technology and software to effectively organize the office.
- Skillfully manages large quantities of information.
- Professionally represents supervisors.
- Maintains seamless day-to-day functions.
- Makes the coordination of multiple events seem effortless.
- She creates systems to streamline department procedures.

- Keeps scrupulous records.
- Keeps files current and easy to access.
- Skilled in managing electronic files.
- Skillfully manages large quantities of information.
- Executes projects impeccably.
- Keeps the office running seamlessly.
- Coordinates the uncoordinated.

Bonus Superlative Phrase

- If forced to choose between losing this assistant and losing their right arm, managers need to think a while before they decide.

Needs Improvement

- Is too slow to adapt to changing needs of those he supports. Needs to stay a step ahead of those he supports by observing events minute by minute.
- Is not in sync with the needs of her supervisors. Needs to anticipate and meet the needs of supervisors by observation and asking questions.
- Does not see it as his job to keep his supervisors organized, even when they are under major deadlines. Needs to keep his supervisors organized.
- Misplaces documents and records. Needs to develop and implement a more effective system for document retrieval.
- Does not update technical skills. Needs to use cutting-edge technology and software to effectively organize the office.
- Becomes overwhelmed by large quantities of information. Needs to develop systems to manage large quantities of information.

- Does not accurately reflect supervisors when she speaks for them. Needs to confidently speak for the people he represents.
- Day-to-day functions are interrupted by special projects. Needs to maintain routines for seamless day-to-day functions as a foundation for those special projects.
- Does not efficiently coordinate multiple events. Needs to attend training in project management and break each event into tasks.
- Lacks an organized approach to regular tasks. Needs to create systems to streamline procedures.
- Records contain costly errors. Needs a minimum of 99 percent accuracy in maintaining records.
- Loses or takes an inordinate amount of time finding records. Needs to create a system to be able to locate records quickly.
- Files are not current and are difficult to access. Needs to redesign his filing system and file weekly.
- Loses files in the computer. Needs to redesign her electronic filing system.
- Becomes overwhelmed by large quantities of information. Needs to develop an information management system that helps him access and prioritize data.
- Overlooks details in project management. Needs to receive training in project management and implement a project management system.
- Inconsistent in performing recurrent responsibilities. Needs to schedule time and reminders for routine, day-to-day activities.

- Office functions are not smooth or efficient. Needs to develop systems to streamline operations.
- Does not effectively coordinate office functions. Needs to coordinate the various office functions.

COMPUTER SKILLS
Exceptional/Acceptable

- Has mastery of the software his job requires.
- Takes initiative to develop the computer skills required for her job.
- Streamlined several procedures previously performed by hand by computerizing them.
- Practices tutorials to develop skills.
- Has an exceptional understanding of computer operation.
- Keeps computer skills current by attending trade shows and seminars.
- Keeps coworkers using the latest technology.
- Does an outstanding job of diagnosing and solving computer problems.
- Helps the computer phobic become computer fanciers.
- Knows the possibilities and limits of computer technology and avails herself of it for the benefit of the organization.

Bonus Superlative Phrase

- If someone said he invented the Internet, I would believe it.

Needs Improvement

- Has not mastered the software her job requires. Needs to take tutorials and classes to develop computer skills.
- Computer skills remain at base minimum for his job. Needs to take initiative to develop the computer skills for more efficient administration of his job.
- Will perform functions by hand rather than developing computer skills to increase output. Needs to computerize processes to increase productivity.
- Does not have sufficient computer skills for the position. Needs to develop computer skills in the areas of . . .
- Does not keep computer skills current. Needs to attend trade shows and seminars to update skills.
- Does not share computer knowledge. Needs to contribute to keeping the office using the latest technology.
- Does not attempt to troubleshoot computer problems or learn from tech support when they troubleshoot her computer problems. Needs to attempt to solve problems and learn how problems are solved.
- Maintains an air of mystery around computers that intimidates others. Needs to help the computer phobic become computer fanciers.
- Performs functions manually that could best be performed by computer. Needs to use computers effectively.
- Uses computers for operations that are best done manually. Needs to use computers effectively.

COST MANAGEMENT

Exceptional/Acceptable

- Makes maximum use of budget.
- Makes realistic and accurate budget projections.
- Carefully monitors budget.
- Is aware of the impact of decisions on the budget.
- Eliminates waste.
- Accurately projects costs.
- Only approves costs that are justified.
- Effectively accounts for all expenses.
- Focuses on cost-to-profit ratio.
- Discovers and eliminates hidden costs.

Bonus Superlative Phrase

- Spends company funds as if investing for his grandmother.

Needs Improvement

- Could make better use of the budget. Needs to optimize expenditures.
- Actual expenses often exceed projections. Needs to make realistic and accurate budget projections.
- Does not stay on top of expenditures. Needs to carefully monitor the budget.
- Makes spending decisions without considering their impact on the budget. Needs to be aware of the impact of spending decisions on the budget.
- Has budget leaks that need to be plugged. Needs to eliminate waste.
- Tends to underestimate actual project costs. Needs to accurately project costs.

- Has trouble saying no to budget requests. Needs to decline approval of costs that are not justified.
- Has accounting gaps for unaccounted expenses. Needs to effectively account for all expenses.
- Projects do not optimize the cost-to-profit ratio. Needs to seek ways to enhance the bottom line and cost-to-profit ratio.
- Overlooks hidden costs. Needs to discover and eliminate hidden costs.

CUSTOMER RELATIONS
Exceptional/Acceptable
- Builds loyal relationships with customers.
- Has built a loyal customer base.
- Clearly loves people and relates well.
- Takes ownership of customer concerns and problems.
- Sounds happy to be speaking with clients.
- Stays positive when dealing with difficult customers.
- If she can't solve a customer's problem, she personally connects them with someone who can.
- Takes a genuine interest in customers.
- Reflects well on our organization when dealing with customers.

Bonus Superlative Phrase
- Makes customers feel like family.

Needs Improvement
- Is impersonal with customers. Needs to develop loyal relationships with customers.

- Spends too much time looking for new customers at the expense of maintaining existing customers. Needs to build a loyal customer base.
- Acts as if customers are an interruption to his other work. Needs to see customer relations as an important part of her job.
- Deflects customer concerns. Needs to take ownership of customer concerns and problems.
- Talks to clients in a cool, impersonal tone. Needs to add warmth to her vocal tone to sound happy to be speaking with clients.
- When customers get irritated with him, he gets irritated back. Needs to stay positive when dealing with difficult customers.
- If she can't solve a customer's problem, she takes no responsibility for helping them find someone who can. Needs to help customers find the right person to help them solve their problems.
- Appears disinterested in customers. Needs to take an interest in them.
- Does not represent the company image when dealing with customers. Needs to realize that he is the company for the customers he deals with and to reflect our organizational values of professionalism, integrity, and quality.

DATA ENTRY
Exceptional/Acceptable

- Enters data fast and accurately.
- Keeps current with data entry.

- Uses good judgment in interpretation of data when necessary.
- Enters data for long periods without tiring.
- Enters data without error.

Bonus Superlative Phrase

- Olympic-level data entry genius, coming in at eleven on a ten-point scale.

Needs Improvement

- Accuracy is good, but speed is slower than average. Needs to practice speed drills to increase speed.
- Misjudges when interpreting data. Needs to take more time to reduce misjudgments.
- Gets behind on data entry. Needs to set a time each day to enter data in order to keep current.
- Tires quickly while entering data. Needs to take short, quick breaks to increase stamina.
- Speed is good but accuracy is below average. Needs to practice drills to increase accuracy.

JOB KNOWLEDGE

Exceptional/Acceptable

- Knows her job well and performs it as a role model.
- Took his job description and performed it to the next level.
- Expanded her job to its true potential.
- Understands and excels at all aspects of his job.
- Is technically skilled at every aspect of her job.
- Understands all procedures relevant to his job.
- Knows whom to contact to get things done quickly.

- Takes the initiative to enhance job skills.
- Sets boundaries when outside demands interfere with job performance.

Bonus Superlative Phrase

- Job knowledge is encyclopedic yet practical.

Needs Improvement

- Does not appear to understand the expectations of his job.
- Seems limited by her job description. Needs to use the job description as a baseline to springboard off of.
- Does not take advantage of opportunities outside of his job description.
- Does not take ownership of all of her job responsibilities. Needs to study her job description and budget appropriate time for every responsibility.
- Lacks technical skills in the following areas . . . Needs to develop these skills.
- Does not follow standard operating procedures. Needs to study and observe procedures relevant to his job.
- Has not created a network of coworkers to get things done quickly. Needs to take the initiative to introduce herself around to discover whom to contact to get things done quickly.
- Does not take the initiative to enhance skills. Needs to practice tutorials and request training.
- Allows unauthorized requests to distract him from job performance. Needs to set boundaries by diplomatically declining unauthorized demands that interfere with job performance.

NEGOTIATION

Exceptional/Acceptable

- Masterfully finds solutions that work for both parties.
- Understands what the other party needs better than they do.
- Skillfully identifies low-cost concessions that have high value for the other party.
- Communicates offers in an appealing way, emphasizing benefits.
- Maintains trust and goodwill through negotiations while keeping the company's interests clearly in mind.
- Does appropriate research on both sides' issues to increase understanding of alternative solutions.
- Recognizes and redirects manipulative negotiating tactics.
- Remains confident when faced with aggressive negotiators.
- Brings the other party to commitment.
- Takes calculated risks to maximize benefits.
- Finds mutually rewarding solutions by expanding the pie/deal.

Bonus Superlative Phrase

- Gets all parties to "yes."

Needs Improvement

- Focuses on his own needs to the exclusion of the needs of the other party. Needs to seek solutions that work for both parties.

- Does not sufficiently research the needs and perspectives of the other party. Needs to understand what the other party needs better than they do.
- Gives best offer at the outset, giving her nowhere to go. Needs to identify low-cost concessions that have high value for the other party to sweeten the deal during negotiation.
- Overemphasizes features and omits benefits in offers. Needs to communicate offers in appealing ways, emphasizing benefits.
- He maintains an aggressive approach that creates defensiveness in the other party. Needs to take the position of collaborator and maintain trust and goodwill through negotiations while keeping the company's interests clearly in mind.
- Falls into the traps of others' negotiating tactics. Needs to recognize and redirect manipulative negotiating tactics.
- Becomes intimidated by aggressive negotiating tactics. Needs to remain confident when faced with aggressive negotiators.
- Misses opportunities to close the discussion. Needs to bring the other party to commitment when the other party starts to send "buying signals."
- Plays it too safe. Is unwilling to risk losing a deal and as a result, makes too many concessions. Needs to take calculated risks to maximize benefits.
- Does not consider options outside the ones on the table. Needs to find mutually rewarding solutions by creatively exploring options that expand the pie/deal.

PHONE SKILLS

Exceptional/Acceptable

- Has an appropriate balance of small talk to business content in conversations.
- Is clear and concise in phone conversations.
- Gives callers her full attention.
- Quickly engages callers or person called.
- Creates an agenda for phone conversations to make best use of time.
- Runs business calls like effective meetings.
- Successfully focuses callers who are unclear.
- Follows up on all calls.
- Keeps excellent records of phone calls for subsequent reference.
- Effectively handles callers who must be placed on hold.
- Handles angry callers with grace and ease.
- Uses the company greeting in a pleasant and effective way.
- Understands and effectively applies the features of the phone system.

Bonus Superlative Phrase

- Her phone style is the highlight of a customer's day.

Needs Improvement

- Sounds impersonal on the phone. Needs to include individual comments that convey warmth in conversations.
- Rambles in phone conversations. Needs to be more focused and concise on the phone.

- Divides attention by doing other things such as checking e-mail and filing while on the phone. Needs to give callers his full attention.

- Is impersonal with callers. Needs to engage callers or person called.

- Does not plan for phone conversations. Needs to create an agenda for phone conversations to make best use of time.

- Is unprepared for and will miss phone appointments. Needs to prepare for and respect phone appointments in the same way as face-to-face meetings.

- Allows callers to ramble without attempting to focus them. Needs to develop questions to focus callers who are unclear.

- Does not follow up on calls in a timely manner. Needs to return all calls within twenty-four hours and follow up on calls.

- Does not keep track of calls. Needs to develop a system to keep records of phone calls for subsequent reference.

- Leaves callers on hold without checking back for three minutes or more. Needs to reconnect every minute with callers to apprise them of the status of their inquiry.

- Does not use an appropriate greeting when answering the phone. Needs to use the company greeting in a pleasant and inviting way.

- Use of company greeting sounds forced and unnatural. Needs to practice the greeting to make it sound conversational.

- Has not learned the capabilities of the phone system.

Needs to study and master the features of the phone system.

PLANNING

Exceptional/Acceptable

- Develops solid action plans.
- Plans own workload in coordination with organizational goals and priorities.
- Anticipates and plans for future demand.
- Invests time in planning daily.
- Plans for contingencies.
- Plans are practical and ready to implement.
- Formulates plans that consider and include all stakeholders.
- Adapts plans as reality dictates.

Bonus Superlative Phrase

- She plans backward and forward and inside out to prepare for all possible avenues and events.

Needs Improvement

- Does not create action plans. Needs to allot a minimum of five minutes of planning for every hour of implementation.
- Acts without planning. Needs to plan before taking action.
- Plans own workload independently of organizational goals and priorities. Needs to coordinate own workload planning with organizational goals and priorities.

- Is often caught unprepared for demands when they arise. Needs to anticipate and plan for future demand.
- Is "too busy to plan." Needs to invest time in planning daily.
- Plans for best-case scenario only. Needs to plan for contingencies.
- Plans are idealistic. Needs to plan realistically with implementation in mind.
- Plans do not consider all stakeholders. Needs to verify plans with other stakeholders before finalizing.
- Sticks to original plan even when events indicate the need to change. Needs to adapt plans as reality dictates.

PRESENTATIONS

Exceptional/Acceptable

- Presentations are clear and have impact.
- Makes lively, enjoyable presentations.
- Presentations hold audience's attention.
- Presentations are well-prepared, organized, and developed.
- Presentations get the audience involved.
- Illustrates points effectively.
- His presentations influence the audience by focusing on benefits as well as features.
- Presentations inspire audiences to action.
- Speaks like a professional.
- Presentations focus on results.

Bonus Superlative Phrase

- Could make the phone book sound exciting with her captivating presentation style.

Needs Improvement

- Presentations are disorganized and lack impact. Needs to outline presentations for greater organization.
- Presentations are factually accurate but dry. Needs to have more fun, so we do, too.
- Has a stiff, clinical style that does not hold audience's attention. Needs to change topics and activities every seven minutes.
- Attempts to be spontaneous in presentations come across as disorganized. Needs to prepare, organize, and practice the presentation.
- Speaks at the audience and does not involve them. Needs to use questions and audience interaction to bring spontaneity.
- Points are abstract and general. Needs to make points clearer with the use of illustrations, examples, and stories.
- Presentations are inspiring but do not result in change or action because of the lack of clear action steps. Needs to provide clear benefits and application steps to inspire action.
- Presentations lack polish. Needs to train in speaking skills and practice presentations before delivering them.
- Presentations inspire but do not cause change. Needs to focus on results and provide action steps in presentations.

PROBLEM SOLVING

Exceptional/Acceptable

- Identifies problems at their inception and analyzes them quickly to find a solution.
- Does not create problems for others.
- Solves problems at their root cause.
- Solves problems before they become major.
- Carefully weighs pros and cons in every decision.
- Anticipates problems and finds solutions before the problem develops.
- Is not thrown off by problems but immediately looks for solutions.
- Sees problems as challenges and opportunities.
- Knows which problems to solve herself and which problems to delegate to subordinates and subject experts.
- Offers a variety of possible solutions for problems.

Bonus Superlative Phrase

- Solves small problems instantly; impossible problems may take a few minutes.

Needs Improvement

- Ignores problems until they become too big to ignore. Needs to address problems sooner.
- Forwards work that contains problems for others to solve. Needs to anticipate and solve problems before passing projects to others.
- Attempts to solve problems by treating symptoms rather than addressing their root causes. Needs to solve problems at their root causes.

- Waits for problems to become critical before solving them. Needs to address problems at their inception.
- Does not consider a sufficiently broad range of information in problem solving. Needs to carefully weigh all pros and cons in every decision.
- Overlooks foreseeable problems. Needs to anticipate problems and find solutions before the problems develop.
- Wallows in problems by denial, resistance, and complaining before looking for solutions. Needs to recognize the opportunities in problems and immediately look for solutions.
- Sees problems as a barrier and does not consider options to resolve them. Needs to approach problems as an opportunity.
- Overmanages by solving problems that would be better to delegate. Needs to determine which problems to solve herself and which problems to delegate to subordinates and subject experts.
- Brings single solutions to problems. Needs to create a broader range of solutions.

PRODUCTIVITY

Exceptional/Acceptable

- Gets more done in a day than most people get done in a week.
- Sets the bar higher for the rest of the team.
- Consistently completes large quantities of work.
- Has an exceptionally high output.
- If we want it done, we give it to him.

- Exceeds performance expectations.
- Completes work ahead of deadlines.
- Uses time in an effective and productive way.
- Uses peak energy times for highest-priority work.
- Creates uninterrupted work periods for maximum productivity.
- Focuses on attaining results in all her activities.

Bonus Superlative Phrase

- Gets a week's worth of work out of a twenty-four-hour day.

Needs Improvement

- Does not produce as much as other workers. Needs to increase output.
- Productivity is inconsistent. Needs to be more consistent to get more done.
- Productivity is below standard. Needs to increase output to meet productivity standards.
- She is not our first choice for important projects that need to be done quickly. Needs to be more consistent in productivity.
- Does not meet productivity expectations. Needs to increase productivity to meet standards.
- Completes work after deadlines. Needs to increase productivity to meet deadlines.
- Wastes time by not batching activities. Needs to organize his day to perform similar tasks in batches to make better use of his time.
- Does not schedule tasks according to productivity cycles. Needs to use peak energy and productivity times for highest-priority work.

- Productivity is diminished by unnecessary interruptions. Needs to create uninterrupted work periods for maximum productivity.
- Does not focus on action steps or results. Needs to
  concentrate on results in all her activities.

PROGRAMMING SKILLS

Exceptional/Acceptable

- Designs programs that address and meet the needs
  of employees or managers.
- Designs programs that are easy to learn and that
  streamline operations.
- Designs programs that are bug-free.
- Designs code that is easy to understand and update.
- Anticipates need for programming projects and ini-
  tiates projects that address the issues.
- Develops code that is easy for other programmers to
  read and interpret.

Bonus Superlative Phrase

- Like Burger King, he does it (designs programs)
  your way.

Needs Improvement

- Programs are not designed with the end user clearly
  in mind. Needs to research, address, and meet the
  needs of employees.
- Programs are complex and difficult to learn. Needs
  to simplify program design.
- Programs are released with bugs. Needs to test
  programs more thoroughly in advance of release to
  minimize bugs.

- Not proactive in initiating programming projects that address issues and meet emerging needs. Needs to anticipate need for programming projects and initiate projects that address the issues.
- Programs are written in complex codes that even other programmers have difficulty understanding. Needs to design code that is easy to understand and update.

PROJECT MANAGEMENT
Exceptional/Acceptable

- Has a mastery of project management software.
- Coordinates resources for projects seamlessly.
- Effectively sets and meets goals, objectives, and milestones.
- Sets appropriate timetables that keep projects moving without creating undue pressure.
- Delivers projects on schedule.
- Delivers projects on budget.
- Effectively updates stakeholders on project progress and results.
- Coordinates communication among stakeholders and project team members.
- Writes effective project reports so recommendations and significant information are easy to access.
- Handles problems that arise in a timely manner.

Bonus Superlative Phrase

- Don't tell NASA about her project-management skills, or they'll want her to manage the Mars mission.

Needs Improvement

- Has minimal understanding of project management software. Needs to receive training to upgrade skills.
- Does not effectively coordinate project resources. Needs to review the project as a whole when allocating resources.
- Timetables do not accommodate all interdependencies. Needs to set goals, objectives, and milestones that reflect and coordinate interdependencies.
- Sets unrealistically optimistic timetables, creating missed deadlines. Needs to set appropriate timetables that keep the project moving without creating undue pressure.
- Sets unrealistically cautious timetables, resulting in inefficiency and prolonged timelines. Needs to set appropriate timetables that keep the project moving without creating undue pressure.
- Misses deadlines. Needs to set more realistic deadlines or increase efficiency.
- Projects come in over budget. Needs to deliver projects on budget.
- Team members and stakeholders do not get sufficient updates. Needs to effectively update stakeholders and team members on project progress and results.
- Inadequate communication among stakeholders and project team members. Needs to coordinate communication among stakeholders and project team members.
- Project reports are incomplete and difficult to access. Needs to write project reports where recommendations and significant information are easy to access.

- Does not handle problems that arise in a timely manner. Needs to immediately address problems, seeking quick, appropriate solutions.

QUALITY OF WORK
Exceptional/Acceptable

- Is committed to quality.
- Work is remarkably error-free.
- Quality of work is consistently high.
- Is committed to excellence.
- Develops systems that assure quality work.
- Quality of work is an inspiration for others.
- Is accurate, effective, and precise.
- Catches flaws others miss.
- Work demonstrates the highest of standards.
- Work inspires excellence in others.
- Maintains high standards even with tight deadlines.

Bonus Superlative Phrase

- For him, quality began on the inside and worked its way out.

Needs Improvement

- Lacks commitment to quality. Needs to aim higher.
- Makes more than a reasonable number of errors. Needs to reduce error rate by double-checking her work.
- Quality of work lacks consistency. Needs to stay alert to errors.
- Quality of work is at a marginal level; he seems willing to accept a less than optimal standard of quality.

Needs to set a higher standard for herself and other project participants.

- Bypasses operating procedures that ensure quality. Needs to follow existing operating procedures and develop additional systems that assure quality work.
- Quality of work is below average. Needs to study and implement procedures of those with better quality records.
- Mistakes have caused work stoppage. Needs to maintain quality to avoid work stoppages.
- Misses flaws others notice. Needs to be more attentive.
- Errors have cost business. Needs to determine causes of errors and implement remedies.
- Work does not inspire excellence in others. Needs to take the lead in modeling excellence.
- Sacrifices quality in tight deadlines. Needs to maintain high standards even with tight deadlines.

RESEARCH

Exceptional/Acceptable

- Has compelling background information and data for every point he makes.
- Research efforts are thorough, effective, and accurate.
- Can make sense of complex data.
- Knows how to locate and interpret relevant data.
- Identifies and applies cutting-edge information relevant to operations.
- Research is impeccable.
- Summarizes research in powerful and understandable reports.

Bonus Superlative Phrase

• She is the Madame Curie of our industry.

Needs Improvement

• Makes unsubstantiated claims. Needs to offer compelling background information and data for every point he makes.

• Research efforts are incomplete and misleading. Needs to be more thorough, effective, and accurate.

• Gets overloaded by complex data. Needs to maintain an awareness of research objectives and to prioritize information.

• Does not exhaust potential sources of data. Needs to be more thorough in research efforts.

• Misses cutting-edge information relevant to operations. Needs to be more current and thorough in research efforts.

• Research reports contain errors and spurious conclusions. Needs to subject reports to rigorous fact-checking prior to submission.

• Research reports are laborious and confusing. Needs to summarize research in powerful and understandable reports.

RESOURCEFULNESS

Exceptional/Acceptable

• Makes excellent use of both people and material resources.

• Finds surprising sources of information and resources.

- Finds ways to save money and resources without compromising outcome.
- Makes outstanding use of available resources.
- Accurately anticipates resources needed to avoid waste or shortage.
- Respects resource needs of other employees and departments while meeting her own resource needs.

Bonus Superlative Phrase

- More resourceful than Heloise.

Needs Improvement

- Seeks additional resources when available resources would meet his needs. Needs to use available resources before requesting more.
- Overlooks sources of information and resources. Needs to continually inventory available resources and use them.
- Incurs unnecessary expenses. Needs to be more aggressive in finding ways to save money and resources.
- Money-saving efforts cost more in productivity and output than savings. Needs to perform cost-benefit analysis of the price versus the value of savings.
- Miscalculates resource needs, resulting in waste. Needs to accurately anticipate resource needs to avoid waste.
- Miscalculates resource needs resulting in shortages. Needs to accurately anticipate resource needs to avoid shortages.

- Uses resources designated for others. Needs to respect the resource needs of other employees and departments while meeting her own resource needs.

SALES

Exceptional/Acceptable

- Knows how to describe benefits in compelling ways.
- Wins the trust of prospective buyers.
- Understands and effectively addresses client needs.
- Meets and exceeds sales goals.
- Closes sales by uncovering any and all reasons for his prospects to buy.
- Can see and express reasons to buy hidden in objections, and overcomes them.
- Wins sales through pleasant persistence.
- Uses great openings and closings.
- Has the ability to gracefully persuade a person into a win-win situation without manipulation.
- Has superb timing in the sales process.
- Knows what customers need better than they do, and sells them what they really need, gets them to spend more than they expected to, and be happy for it.
- Creates new customers through cold calls, referrals, and excellent customer relations.
- Manages time and territory with efficiency.

Bonus Superlative Phrase

- She is a lean, mean, and squeaky clean sales machine.

Needs Improvement

- Focuses on features to the exclusion of benefits. Needs to describe benefits in compelling ways.

- Comes across as pushy and as more interested in making a sale than addressing the interests of the client. Needs to work to win the trust of prospective buyers.

- Sales approach seems "one size fits all." Needs to understand and effectively address client needs.

- Sales do not meet goals. Needs to increase sales by _____ percent.

- Loses sales by overlooking customer needs that our product meets. Needs to uncover any and all reasons for his prospects to buy and to close the sale.

- Argues against or is discouraged by customer objections rather than exploring and explaining how our products meet their needs. Needs to see objections as the reason to buy, and overcome them.

- Gives up at early signs of disinterest. Needs to be pleasantly persistent.

- Does not capture customer interest with powerful opening remarks. Needs to develop openings.

- Does not clearly ask for the sale. Needs to develop and apply closing statements that clearly ask for the sale.

- Overlooks customer signals and does not adapt sales script to customer needs. Needs to adjust timing in script to customer signals.

- Does not research or anticipate customer needs. Loses sales by not addressing all legitimate needs. Needs to understand customers' needs better than they do.

- Number of cold calls is below average. Needs to increase cold calls by _____ percent. Needs to create new customers through cold calls.
- Does not ask for referrals. Needs to build customer base through referrals.
- Loses customers through neglect. Needs to nourish customer base.

18

Professionalism

The phrases in this chapter will help you describe performance regarding professionalism. These phrases are the summary phrases to be used in Step 3 of the five steps of performance review mastery detailed in chapter 3 and summarized in the beginning of chapter 15, page 107. Please review these pages to understand the context these phrases are intended to be used in before proceeding. The beginning of chapter 15 also explains the use of exceptional versus acceptable phrases, bonus superlatives, and the use of phrases to create a development plan.

ACHIEVEMENT

Exceptional/Acceptable

- He makes things happen.
- She gets concrete results.
- He targets outcome.
- Knows the difference between action and results.
- Uses time for powerful results.
- She surpasses expectations.
- He consistently moves out of his league to higher levels.

Bonus Superlative Phrase

• When she sets her sight on things, hold on to your hat.

Needs Improvement

• He seems dependent on others to makes things happen. Needs to be more self-reliant and results oriented.

• Results are abstract and difficult to measure. Needs to focus on concrete results.

• She lacks focus on goals. She needs to target outcome.

• Creates an appearance of being busy and seems to think that busyness is enough without results. Needs to know the difference between action and results.

• Does not focus on results or completion. Needs to target concrete measurable goals for powerful results.

• Does not meet achievement expectations. Needs to increase output.

• Seems content to stay where he is. Needs to move out of his league to higher levels.

ALIGNMENT WITH MISSION

Exceptional/Acceptable

• Knows the company mission and uses it to guide actions and decisions.

• Makes decisions based on mission.

• Sets goals based on mission.

• Inspires others to value mission.

- Incorporates mission into every meeting.
- Aligns employee objectives with mission.

Bonus Superlative Phrase

- It's not a job for this employee, it's a mission.

Needs Improvement

- Does not maintain an awareness of the company mission. Needs to refer to mission.
- Decisions do not reflect mission. Needs to refer to the mission in decision making.
- Goals do not reflect mission. Needs to refer to the mission in goal setting.
- Does not mention mission in communication. Needs to refer to the mission and inspire others to value it.
- Allows employees to operate tactically rather than strategically. Needs to align employee objectives with company mission.

DEADLINES

Exceptional/Acceptable

- Can be trusted to meet all deadlines.
- Brings projects in ahead of deadlines.
- Works well under pressure.
- Budgets time to allow for delays.
- If he promises to get something done by a specified time, he does.
- Sets deadlines for herself that are challenging yet realistic.

- Maintains high standards, even with tight deadlines.
- Coordinates and manages work with others to assure timelines are met.

Bonus Superlative Phrase

- Sets deadlines to turn dreams into reality.

Needs Improvement

- Treats deadlines as suggestions rather than imperatives. Needs to take deadlines seriously.
- Brings projects in late. Needs to create project management timelines to meet project deadlines.
- Loses focus under pressure. Needs to apply stress management tools and self-discipline to maintain focus.
- Budgets time based on best-case scenario. Needs to budget time cushions to allow for delays.
- Takes deadlines lightly. Needs to back up all promises with action.
- Does not set deadlines to pace work flow, resulting in work jams. Needs to set deadlines for tasks within projects.
- Sets generous deadlines that do not move work forward expediently. Needs to set deadlines for herself that are challenging yet realistic.
- Sets strident deadlines that are unrealistic. Needs to set deadlines for himself that are challenging yet realistic.
- Sacrifices quality in tight deadlines. Needs to maintain high standards even with tight deadlines.

DEPENDABILITY

Exceptional/Acceptable

- Delivers as promised.
- Says what she will do, and does what she says.
- Can be counted on to pitch in when needed.
- Sees projects and responsibilities through to completion.
- Meets deadlines.
- Says what he means. Can be taken at his word.
- Is always prepared.

Bonus Superlative Phrase

- Is more dependable than gravity.

Needs Improvement

- Misses deadlines. Needs to budget time to assure timely completion of projects.
- Is vague in making commitments so it becomes difficult to know what to count on. Needs to specifically say what she will do and to do what she says.
- Is limited by the job description and rarely can be counted on to pitch in as needed. Needs to pitch in when needed.
- Needs careful supervision to get things done. Needs to see projects and responsibilities through to completion on his initiative.
- Promises are often broken. Needs to say what she means and can commit to.
- Is often unprepared. Needs to prepare well in advance.

EFFICIENCY

Exceptional/Acceptable

- Knows the shortest distance between two points and takes it.
- Has efficiency down to a fine art.
- Streamlines processes to their most efficient execution.
- Does more with less.
- Finds the quickest way to get things done.
- Uses technology to streamline procedures.
- Eliminates waste in processes and procedures.

Bonus Superlative Phrase

- So efficient the job is almost done as soon as he starts.

Needs Improvement

- Does not use time well. Needs to determine the shortest distance between two points and take it.
- Uses inefficient methods and processes. Needs to develop efficiency.
- Does not look for more efficient ways to execute. Needs to streamline processes to their most efficient execution.
- Does not look for ways to do more with less. Needs to find ways to get better results with fewer resources.
- Uses outdated procedures that take longer than expected. Needs to find the quickest way to get things done.

- Is reluctant to develop technical skills. Needs to use technology to streamline procedures.
- Work habits and procedures include waste. Needs to eliminate unnecessary steps to streamline processes and procedures.

ETHICS

Exceptional/Acceptable

- Is scrupulously honest.
- Is high-minded.
- Does not compromise ethics for expediency.
- Makes the right choice even if she could get away with making an unethical choice.
- Demonstrates integrity.
- Never bends the truth.
- Admits responsibility for errors and takes actions to correct the problems they cause.

Bonus Superlative Phrase

- When choosing between the right thing and the easy thing, he chooses the right thing and makes it easy.

Needs Improvement

- Sometimes bends the truth. Needs to strive to a higher level of honesty.
- Appears to have an "end-justifies-the-means" mindset. Needs to take the high road.
- Compromises ethics for expediency. Needs to avoid shortcuts that do not reflect well on her and the company.

- Will mislead by speaking in a way that is literally true but deceptive. Needs to take responsibility for the accuracy of his message.
- Makes the wrong choice believing she can get away with taking an unethical shortcut. Needs to make the same ethical choice whether she can get away with an unethical shortcut or not.

FINANCIAL MANAGEMENT
Exceptional/Acceptable

- Understands how to interpret numbers and makes on-target analysis.
- Monitors expenses and income, providing guidance and warning to management when necessary.
- Has devised systems to monitor expenses and income.
- Makes sure standing cash is producing appropriate interest.
- Presents reports to management that are understandable and helpful for making decisions.
- Manages finances to the company objectives.
- Presents realistic budgets after working closely with department heads.

Bonus Superlative Phrase

- Manages money so well I would trust him with my mother's retirement account.

Needs Improvement

- Offers no or little interpretation or analysis of our numbers. Needs training to learn to understand how to interpret our numbers and make on-target analysis.

- Lets expenses outstrip income, putting the company in negative financial situations. Needs to diligently monitor expenses and income, providing guidance and warning to management when necessary.
- Lacks routines or systems to monitor expenses and income. Must devise systems to monitor expenses and income.
- Doesn't place money in instruments to provide the best interest. Needs to make sure our standing cash is producing appropriate interest.
- Presents reports to management that are confusing and not useful. Needs to present understandable reports that are helpful for making decisions.

FOCUS

Exceptional/Acceptable

- Focuses well, even when there are many diversions.
- Zeros in on what she needs to do.
- Has a remarkable ability to concentrate.
- Keeps his eye on the goal.
- Homes in on key details.
- Is able to decipher which items are most important and get them completed first.
- Diplomatically negotiates changes in deadlines of less important tasks/projects in order to stay focused on first-priority ones.
- Is able to maintain focus even when task is tedious and laborious.

Bonus Superlative Phrase

- Could focus even if Mount Vesuvius was erupting.

Needs Improvement

- Attention is fragmented between numerous tasks. Needs to focus on one thing at a time.
- Does not stay focused on priorities. Needs to zero in on important versus urgent activities.
- Has difficulty focusing. Needs to remove distractions to concentrate.
- Gets distracted and loses sight of the goal. Needs to create and prioritize a task list daily and revisit it throughout the day.
- Misses key details. Needs to brainstorm all possibilities in writing and focus on the most relevant details.
- Focuses on whatever task was most recently presented. Needs to be able to decipher which items are most important and get them completed first.
- Has a hard time staying on task when others are around. Needs to be able to focus well, even when there are many diversions, by taking work to a quieter location and telling people who are interrupting that she needs to focus.
- Focuses work efforts on the task for the person who complains the loudest. Needs to be able to diplomatically negotiate changes in deadlines of less important tasks/projects in order to stay focused on first-priority ones.
- Stops work mid-task or mid-project if the work is tedious and laborious. Needs to maintain focus through to task completion, even when task is tedious and laborious.

GOAL ACHIEVEMENT/SETTING

Exceptional/Acceptable

- Sets goals on a quarterly, monthly, weekly, and daily basis to guide work.
- Uses goals to enhance achievement.
- Goals reflect the mission and objectives of the organization.
- Uses goals to prioritize tasks.
- Sets goals that are challenging yet achievable, and achieves them.
- Sets goals that are concrete and measurable for accountability.
- Communicates goals in a way that inspires others to support him to achieve them.
- Sets challenging goals and meets them.
- Sets personal goals in alignment with department and company goals.

Bonus Superlative Phrase

- Wins the gold medal for accomplishing Olympic-level goals.

Needs Improvement

- Does not set goals. Needs to set goals on a quarterly, monthly, weekly, and daily basis to guide work.
- Does not use goals to create focus. Needs to use goals to enhance achievement.
- Goals are not in alignment with the company mission. Needs for goals to reflect the mission and objectives of the organization.

- Does not have a clear idea of what needs to be done. Needs to use goals to prioritize tasks.
- Goals lack challenge. Needs to set goals that are challenging yet achievable, and achieve them.
- Goals are unrealistic. Needs to set goals that are achievable yet challenging, and achieve them.
- Goals are vague and not measurable. Needs to set goals that are concrete and measurable for accountability.
- Keeps goals to himself. Needs to communicate goals in a way that inspires others to support him to achieve them.
- Fails to meet baseline goals. Needs to create a plan, track progress, and meet the baseline goals as a foundation to setting and achieving more challenging goals.
- Daily activities do not advance department goals. Needs to set daily goals in alignment with department and company goals.

GROOMING
Exceptional/Acceptable
- Looks professional.
- Appearance reflects positively on the organization.
- Grooming is flawless.
- Appearance projects a positive impression.
- Grooming is always appropriate for the occasion.

Bonus Superlative Phrase
- Grooming is so impeccable, the rumor is she is digitally enhanced.

Needs Improvement

- Has taken business casual to an extreme. Needs to dress more professionally.
- Appearance does not reflect positively on the organization. Needs to groom with the awareness that he represents the organization.
- Does not pay attention to detail in grooming. Needs to upgrade shoes, hair, and accessories to project professionalism.
- Appearance does not project a positive image. Needs to upgrade attire to appear more professional.
- Does not adapt dress to the occasion. Needs to consider clients and function when choosing attire.

LEADERSHIP

Exceptional/Acceptable

- Effectively offers clear directions that others follow in unison.
- Provides an inspiring vision that motivates others.
- Inspires loyalty from others.
- Involves others in leading.
- Uses authority without dictating.
- Is a role model for others.

Bonus Superlative Phrase

- Inspires such high-level performance, employees look forward to their performance reviews.

Needs Improvement

- Does not provide a clear direction. Needs to communicate her direction in a clear, actionable format.

- Does not communicate his vision convincingly. Needs to develop a practical, clear message and a plan to convey it through consistent repetition.
- Does not provide a vision for employees to move toward. Needs to provide an inspiring vision for others to follow.
- Does not create a sense of loyalty among employees. Needs to inspire loyalty by supporting employees.
- Does not involve others in leading. Needs to empower others by delegating leadership functions.
- Comes across as autocratic. Needs to use persuasive authority rather than power-based authority.
- Is reluctant to lead. Needs to make tough decisions, hold people accountable, and set standards.
- Attempts to lead by telling people what to do rather than showing them. Needs to be a role model for others.

LOGICAL THINKING
Exceptional/Acceptable

- Analyzes situations logically.
- Does not let emotion override reason.
- Makes sense of complex situations.
- Interprets data and comes to logical conclusions.
- Uses piercing insight to comprehend the essence of a message or a situation.
- Balances logic with intuition for accurate understanding.

Bonus Superlative Phrase

- So logical he makes Sir Isaac Newton seem like Elmer Fudd.

Needs Improvement

- Draws conclusions that are not supported by the facts. Needs to analyze situations logically.
- Allows emotion to override reason and confuse the facts. Needs to set emotions aside in evaluating situations.
- Develops overly simplistic analysis of complex situations. Needs to take the time to comprehend complex situations.
- Misinterprets data and comes to unsupported conclusions. Needs to use data to come to logical conclusions.
- Misses the essence of a message. Needs to focus more deeply on the essence of a message.
- Makes logical arguments that are counterintuitive and later proven wrong. Needs to balance logic with intuition.

LOYALTY

Exceptional/Acceptable

- Is loyal to the success and mission of the organization.
- Supports the mission and goals of the organization.
- Is very dedicated.
- Contributing to the organizational mission is a high priority.
- Speaks highly of the company to others.

- Represents the organization well in all situations at all times.

Bonus Superlative Phrase
- More loyal than Lassie.

Needs Improvement
- Places personal goals ahead of company goals. Needs to display loyalty to the success and mission of the organization.
- Is unaware of the mission and goals of the organization. Needs to support the mission and goals of the organization.
- Speaks negatively about the organization in public. Needs to seek understanding of business rationale to present a more accurate and positive image of the company in public.
- Works to meet personal needs over organizational needs. Needs to make contributing to the organizational mission a high priority.

MOTIVATION
Exceptional/Acceptable
- Is highly motivated.
- Works on projects with an excited gusto.
- Has a powerful sense of purpose.
- Translates ideas into action without hesitation.
- Is inspired to take action.
- She is motivated from within.
- He works with enthusiasm.

- Comes in early and leaves late, not because she has to, but because she wants to.
- His enthusiasm is contagious.
- I never have to build a fire under her because the fire is burning inside her.

Bonus Superlative Phrase

- Goes from zero to sixty in three seconds.

Needs Improvement

- Requires incentives to perform. Needs more self-motivation.
- Works on projects at a lackluster pace. Needs to increase personal motivation.
- Does not work with a purpose in mind. Needs to develop a sense of purpose.
- Motivated to create ideas, but lacks motivation to take those ideas into action. Needs to translate ideas into action.
- Is more talk than action. Needs to translate words into action.
- Responds to incentive programs, but does not appear motivated to act without specific incentives. Needs internal motivation.
- Complains about job assignments. Needs to work with enthusiasm or to negotiate for different assignments.
- Comes in late, watches the clock, and leaves early, even when the workload is high. Needs to focus on the job that needs to be done rather than the clock.

SAFETY

Exceptional/Acceptable

- Follows all safety procedures.
- Has no safety breaches.
- Very conscious of safety practices.
- Promotes safety practices with others.
- Contributes to effective safety procedures.
- Wears all safety equipment.
- Avoids unnecessary risks.
- Careful without being overcautious.

Bonus Superlative Phrase

- So safety-oriented I would want him to pack my parachute.

Needs Improvement

- Bypasses safety procedures. Needs to observe all safety procedures.
- Has (number) safety breaches. Needs to reduce these breaches to none.
- Dismisses safety procedures. Needs to become conscious of safety practices.
- Does not promote safety among others. Needs to promote safety practices with others.
- Does not inform management of the need for additional safety procedures. Needs to contribute to effective safety procedures.
- Does not always wear safety equipment. Needs to follow procedures to wear safety equipment.
- Takes unnecessary risks. Needs to follow safety procedures.

- Uses safety as an excuse for underperformance. Needs to refer to safety policy as her guideline for activities.

TIME MANAGEMENT

Exceptional/Acceptable

- Uses time wisely.
- Budgets time well.
- Manages time according to priorities.
- Does what she needs to do herself, and delegates what is best done by others.
- Plans his time effectively and is not thrown by emergencies.
- Manages time in a consistent manner to avoid burnout.
- Does first things first.
- Divides projects into manageable tasks and schedules activities accordingly.
- Averts problems before they occur to avoid having to fight blazing fires.

Bonus Superlative Phrase

- Squeezes an hour out of a minute.

Needs Improvement

- Spends time on low priorities. Needs to use time wisely.
- Is impulsive in how he spends time, being easily diverted by others. Needs more discipline in focusing on first-priority work until it is completed.

- Does not budget time. Needs to budget time to ensure everything gets the attention it needs.
- Lets low-priority demands overshadow high-priority tasks. Needs to manage time according to priorities.
- Keeps tasks that are best performed by others. Needs to do what she needs to do herself, and delegate what is best done by others.
- Does not plan for emergencies. Needs to allow time in his schedule for emergencies.
- Takes a while to get back on track when emergencies disrupt plans. Needs to create and prioritize a to-do list to have a place to get back on track.
- Works in spurts and burns out. Needs to manage time in a consistent manner to avoid burnout.
- Lack of self-direction, not lack of time, is the problem. Needs to devise ways to manage focus to accomplish what is first priority first.
- Procrastinates performing priority tasks by focusing on lower-value activities. Needs to do first things first.
- His attempts to tackle huge projects all at once result in disorganization. Needs to divide projects into manageable tasks and schedule activities accordingly.
- Avoids addressing problems until they are no longer able to be ignored. Needs to address problems at their inception.

About the Authors

MERYL RUNION

MERYL RUNION, MSCI, CSP, is the president and CEO of SpeakStrong Inc., and managing director of the Center for Responsible Communication. She has helped over 300,000 people speak the simple truth through worldwide seminars, keynotes, workshops, and her weekly e-mail newsletter, *A PowerPhrase a Week*. Her books have sold over 200,000 copies worldwide. Her clients include IBM, Lockheed Martin, and the FBI. Her education includes a B.A. from Vanderbilt University and an MSCI from MERU research university.

RUNION BOOKS

How to Use PowerPhrases to Say What You Mean, Mean What You Say and Get What You Want

Perfect Phrases for Managers and Supervisors

PowerPhrases! The Perfect Words to Say It Right and Get the Results You Want

KEYNOTES AND SEMINARS

The Difference Between Lightning Bugs and Lightning Bolts: *How to Use PowerPhrases to Say What You*

Mean and Mean What You Say—Without Being Mean When You Say It

The "SpeakStrong" Supervisor: *How to Speak So Employees Listen and Listen So Employees Speak*

The Totally Integrated Performance System: *How to Manage Seamlessly*

Conflict as Opportunity: *Getting to the Root and Resolution of Conflict*

NEWSLETTER

You can sign up for the SpeakStrong weekly newsletter at www.speakstrong.com.

CONTACT INFORMATION

Send inquiries to info@SpeakStrong.com. Web addresses: www.centerforresponsiblecommunication.com and www.SpeakStrong.com.

SPEAKSTRONG VISION IN MULTIMEDIA

The SpeakStrong vision can be seen in the Internet movie *A World of Truth* at www.speakstrong.com/movie.html.

POWERPHRASES IN ACTION

PowerPhrases can be seen in action in the entertaining *Legend of Mighty Mouth* at www.speakstrong.com/movie .html.

JANELLE BRITTAIN

JANELLE BRITTAIN, MBA, CSP, is president of the Dynamic Performance Institute, LLC. She holds an executive MBA and is a Certified Speaking Professional, an award from the National Speakers Association, which only 400 people have ever achieved worldwide over the last twenty years. As an internationally known speaker, trainer, consultant, and executive coach, Janelle has helped many Fortune 100 companies, as well as hot entrepreneurial firms, in the many aspects of developing leadership, management, and teams. Her clients span the globe from North America to Africa to Asia.

She is an author of five published books, including the recently published *Star Team Dynamics: 12 Lessons Learned from Experienced Team Builders*. Business publications such as the *Wall Street Journal*, *Investor's Business Daily*, and *Crain's Chicago Business* seek Janelle's insights. Janelle has produced a training video, *Flexible Thinking*, and an audiocassette, *Exceptional Thinking Under Pressure*.

PROGRAMS INCLUDE
- *Managing Performance for Results*
- *Coaching for Improved Performance*
- *Global Team Leadership*
- *Leading Through the Tough Stuff*
- *Coping with Change without Maalox*

CONTACT INFORMATION
Send inquiries to Janelle@DynamicPerformance.com. Web address: www.DynamicPerformance.com.